GLOBETROTTER™

Travel

D0245011

NAPLES
AND SORRENTO

MICHAEL LEECH &
MELISSA SHALES

NEW
HOLLAND

NEW
HOLLAND

★★★ Highly recommended
★★ Recommended
★ See if you can

Second edition published in 2003
by New Holland Publishers (UK) Ltd
London • Cape Town • Sydney • Auckland
First published in 2001
10 9 8 7 6 5 4 3 2 1

website: www.newhollandpublishers.com

Garfield House, 86 Edgware Road
London W2 2EA, United Kingdom

80 McKenzie Street, Cape Town,
8001, South Africa

14 Aquatic Drive, Frenchs Forest,
NSW 2086, Australia

218 Lake Road, Northcote,
Auckland, New Zealand

Distributed in the USA by
The Globe Pequot Press, Connecticut

ISBN 1 84330 499 6

Although every effort has been made to ensure that this
guide is up to date and current at time of going to print,
the Publisher accepts no responsibility or liability for
any loss, injury or inconvenience incurred by readers
or travellers using this guide.

Keep us Current
Information in travel guides is apt to change, which is
why we regularly update our guides. We'd be grateful
to receive feedback if you've noted something we
should include in our updates. If you have new
information, please share it with us by writing to the
Publishing Manager, Globetrotter, at the office nearest

to you (addresses on this page). The most significant
contribution to each new edition will receive a free copy
of the updated guide.

Publishing Manager (UK): Simon Pooley
Publishing Manager (SA): Thea Grobbelaar
DTP Cartographic Manager: Genené Hart
Editors: Melany McCallum, Tarryn Berry
Consultant: Liz Booth
Design and DTP: Lellyn Creamer
Picture Researcher: Colleen Abrahams
Cartographers: Marisa Galloway, Elaine Fick
Proofreader: Ingrid Schneider

Reproduction by Hirt & Carter (Pty) Ltd, Cape Town
Printed and bound in Hong Kong by Sing Cheong
Printing Co. Ltd

Photographic Credits:
Axiom Photographic Agency/Lucy Davies: pp. 41. 85;
Axiom Photographic Agency/D Shaw: p. 11; **Mark
Azavedo Photo Library:** title page, pp. 4, 8, 13, 15, 16,
17, 21, 22, 27, 29, 30, 32, 36, 37, 39, 42, 43, 45, 48, 49, 52,
55, 58, 59, 60, 66, 67, 68, 73, 92, 93, 94, 95, 100, 102, 111,
114, 117, 118, 119; **HL:** pp. 62, 64; **HL/Robert Aberman:**
pp. 23, 25, 28; **HL/Robert Francis:** pp. 6, 7, 9, 10, 72, 110;
Life File/David Kempfner: pp. 26, 46; **Richard Sale:** pp.
88, 98, 105, 106, 107, 108, 109; **SCPL:** p. 12; **SCPL/Ian
Leonard:** pp. 14, 35, 69, 70, 74, 76; **SCPL/ Chris North:**
pp. 34, 56, 57; **SCPL/Chris Parker:** cover, p. 104;
SCPL./Jonathon Smith: p. 18; **SCPL/Jill Swainson:** pp.
80, 82; **SCPL/J Worker:** pp. 40, 47, 90, 103; **Melissa
Shales:** pp. 20, 24, 38, 78, 81, 83.
*(SCPL: Sylvia Cordaiy Photo Library; HL: Hutchison
Library)*

Acknowledgements:
Melissa Shales would like to thank the following
for their help in researching this book: Go Airline;
Alessandra Smith and Michela Moguolo of the Italian
Tourist Office in London for their assistance in planning
the trip; Interhome holiday apartments; Royal-
Continental Hotel, Naples; Grand Hotel Royal, Sorrento;
Excelsior Vittoria Hotel, Sorrento; and Casa Albertina
Hotel, Positano for assistance with accommodation;
Stephen Fowler, as always, for his invaluable assistance
with research; the staff and patients of Nuovi Pellegrini
Hospital, Michael Burgoyne and Rosalba Viggiani of the
British Consulate in Naples for their help.

Front Cover: *The rocky coastline of the Amalfi.*
Title Page: *View of the Bay of Naples with Vesuvius
in the background.*

CONTENTS

1
Introducing
Naples and Sorrento

Naples is a city that resounds to a drum roll of history. For thousands of years, this city, has pursued a double life – enjoying a privileged position beside the Mediterranean – yet in the dangerous proximity of a huge volcano. Throughout recorded history, **Vesuvius** has had long periods of calm, then sudden, often very violent eruptions. The most famous was in AD79 when a cataclysmic explosion sent magma boiling over and superheated air to bury **Pompeii** and **Herculaneum**. Reading contemporary descriptions still chills, and you can see in the now peaceful countryside the recovered ruins of its lost Roman cities.

Naples itself was for centuries a city state, growing rich and powerful under a succession of ruling lords. When Italy became one country in the mid-19th century, decline set in. It is a city of extraordinary contrasts. Easily walked, there are lots of surprises – palaces, castles, churches, the harbour front, gardens and promenades. It also has dark, grim streets and, though much improved of recent years, it remains an overcrowded, pulsing city, yet full of character.

Surrounding the city is the beautiful province of **Campania**, with some of the most famous sights in the world including the **Amalfi Drive** and the **Bay of Naples**, **Capri** and the vast royal palace of **Caserta**. There are numerous sites from antiquity too, and for those who like the simple life, exploration of Campania's rich countryside and villages is recommended for extended drives, walks and visits. Naples has been catering for tourists for centuries, and now that it is losing its dark image of dirt and crime, it should be alluring to even more visitors.

Don't Miss

*** **Pompeii:** freed from a carpet of volcanic ash, a city revealed from antiquity.
*** **Capri:** one of the most beautiful islands in the world.
*** **The Amalfi Drive:** cliffs, sparkling sea, vine framed villages, fishing boats, all seen from a shore-hugging road.
** **Old Naples:** a fascinating tangle of a town, crowded and cheerful.
** **Sorrento:** a perfect little resort town looking across to Capri from its cliff-top perch.
** **Vesuvius:** visit the summit of this amazing live volcano.

Opposite: *Sorrento, ranged along its clifftop, overlooking the clear blue sea.*

Below: *The busy port city of Salerno is a good base for exploring the sites along the Amalfi coast and the Greek city of Paestum.*

THE LAND

The entire west-facing coastal area of Campania faces and slopes toward the sea, quite steeply at first from inland heights, then softening down to coastal hills. The stern backbone of the **Appenine Range**, the central mountain-ous spine running the length of Italy, rises to the east like a protective wall. Effectively creating markedly different east and west regions, it strides down from east of Genoa to Sicily. These often snow topped mountains are of lime-stone, and near the south of Naples, they are subject to earthquakes and volcanic eruptions due to volatile tectonic plate movements. The other principal heights are volcanic. The original substructure and the later volcanic activity of the area results in richly varied scenery.

Limestone forms the lower arm of the two promontories of land that enclose the famous **Bay of Naples**. The bay is a vast saucer of shielded water, a natural harbour. Sculpted into rugged shapes it is also deeply cut and carved, and under the surface are large limestone caverns, some flooded. Along the coasts, the rock is indented by the sea and makes for a series of world famous sights in a ravishing parade of capes, bays, and steep cliffs, some embraced with precipitous small settle-ments. At the foot are tiny beaches, backed by the soft azure of the Mediterranean.

The Volcanic origins of Campania

The area has always floated on a vast sea of hidden volcanic lava, the **Campi Flegrei**. Towering over it, Mount Vesuvius is really just a colossal relief valve that occasionally – although very violently sometimes – relieves in its eruptions the intense pressure building up just a few thousand metres below. The thick shielding layer of limestone caps the vast

magma lake boiling below, and this is the foundation stone of Campania, lying at various depths beneath the whole province. The super hot magma of the Campi Flegrei, relatively close to the surface, means the fostering and eruption of warm sulphurous springs too. These are found on the mainland and are particularly widespread on the island of Ischia.

Vesuvius is one of the most famous volcanoes in the world – dangerous, yet in repose extremely beautiful. The volcano has attracted tourists here for centuries with its infrequent yet often terrifying eruptions. Smoke still hangs lazily above Vesuvius, a warning that the fiery lady may appear quiescent, but is really only sleeping.

The lava, ash and dust fallen to earth from many ancient volcanic eruptions has richly coloured the Campanian soil and fertilized it well over many centuries. This, with the caressing warmth of the climate, has resulted in a mass of vegetation that is lush and green, even in the winter period. Indeed, this rural part of Italy will appeal to those who like to get off the track and explore. You can find here a natural Campania that has altered little, with unchanging hill towns, tiny villages, sometimes tumble-down and impoverished, and farms.

Above: *Tourists visiting Mount Vesuvius feel a great respect for this famous volcano, which could erupt at any moment.*

HIDDEN HELLFIRE

Volcanic action always marks the landscape and life of the region, even if many of the actual fires are long dead, leaving ancient **caldera**. *Campi Flegrei* means 'field of fire', and while this long concealed oven stretching beneath Naples and Cuma is no longer visible, it still makes its presence felt in small **earthquakes** and the many volcanic features of the area. Aside from **hot springs**, it provides spas for bathing in the sulphurous waters and treatments using volcanic mud.

Above: *A view of the Mergellina beach and marina. This bayside suburb contains many popular restaurants.*

Facts and Figures

Campania, one of Italy's smaller provinces, is 13,600 km² (5250 sq miles) in area. Yet it has in **Naples**, one of Italy's major cities, a population of close to 1.5 million. The province is not large, yet it is the second most densely populated area in Italy after Lombardy and the Milan conurbation.

Naples is the second biggest working port in Italy after Genoa, further north in Liguria. The port provides much local employment. It is centrally placed and you can actually drive through it as you enter Naples from the airport and see some of the activity. Or you can go to the quays by the rail station in the city to see it at first hand. Otherwise principal industries are food production and export, (the pasta is notable) engineering, steel works and oil refineries.

The area is very important for its agriculture, with many products benefiting from an early, warm spring. Everyday and exotic fruits predominate, but in its sheltered valleys Campania grows a vast array of vegetables, fruits, nuts, olives, cereals and hemp. A most important industry is that of wine making, and the growing and cultivation of grapes has a very long and important history here. It is depicted in many ways, even, and notably, in frescoes from buried Pompeii. The wine is distinctive with a tang, some say, of volcanic vapours. Tobacco is also grown here – like France, Italy still has a large number of smokers.

Tourism provides a critical income, and there is a good infrastructure especially in the popular areas of Sorrento and the islands, including fair transport by train and road. There are first class restaurants and luxurious hotels of international aspect, some having helicopter terminals. Mount Vesuvius is the highest point at 1281m (4163ft).

Climate

Campania is rarely too hot, and equally, not often cold. Although, it can be quite cool out of the hot months of summer, and even wintry in the eastern hills. At times, however, a sudden chill can descend and cause dank days early in the year. The city itself can be humid, especially in high summer, but breezes from the Mediterranean usually compensate. Rainfall is low.

Afraid you will find Naples too cloying and warm in summer? If the idea of staying in a city during hot periods is not to your taste, consider fresh air at nearby coastal towns, or even go inland. Possibilities (aside from the islands and the scenic areas) are Capua, Salerno, Avellino or Sorrento, which have easy access not only to Naples (a good train system operates) but to the local countryside too.

The Coast

Italy has a coastline more than 7500km (4661 miles) long. The coast of Campania is only a small section of this very long shore

> **MYTHS OF THE MOUNTAINS**
>
> The ancient world looked on the **Bay of Naples** with a special respect. So famous was the beauty and mysterious aspect of the area, allied with the ferocious and unpredictable power of the living volcano, that in classical times it was considered to be a mystical location. The **Lago d'Averno** is really a flooded crater, and its waters are particularly dark, lonely and atmospheric. Birds flying over were often asphyxiated by fumes, and thus it was regarded by both Homer and Virgil as the actual **mouth of the Underworld.**

Below: *The autostrada runs from Naples to the South, passing the outskirts of Salerno.*

COLOURED CAVES

The underlying rock being limestone, a porous and soft rock that is fairly easily worn away, it easily conducts water which in turn excavates and floods it. This ongoing water action results in **tunnels and caverns, stalactites and stalagmites**. Large caves abound along the coastline and on the islands and some are magnificently coloured **blue** or **green**, due to the reflections through the brilliantly clear water. They exist under the city too. Major attractions are the beautiful sea-sculpted **caverns** of Capri and Positano. You should not miss taking a boat trip to explore them.

Below: *The picturesque Amalfi coast is a popular tourist spot.*

which faces four seas – here it is the **Tyrrhenian Sea**. Along with eruptions, and the danger of earthquakes (the last in 1980), the Campanian coast has during all its history been constantly shaped, altered and added to by geological tremors. The stone you will see most of is the white chalky limestone, visible away from the volcano. Successive lava flows have covered it in the vicinity of the mountain, elsewhere it is often worn down by the elements. When it pokes through the green covering of the land, it is like glimpsing the submerged stony skeleton of Campania. Extending west of Naples and forming the edges of the large bite of the Bay of Naples, are two rocky arms of land. Once long peninsulas pointing into the **Mediterranean**, they are now broken at their ends into the islands of Prócida and Ischia to the north, both of volcanic origin, and Capri to the south. Together these two sea-girt extensions of Campania offer the best resorts and form the most famous scenic spots in the whole of Italy.

To the north-west of Naples the coast runs below Capua and Caserta in the hills above, the coastal road passing several seaside towns. This coastline extends to Sessa and the border with the neighbouring province of

Lazio. A much longer stretch of coast runs south-east of the Amalfi coast, starting at Salerno and passing through Paestum, then Agropoli. From this town a secondary road runs south and then east by the sea, going through a number of small resorts and past rocky capes and headlands until it arrives at the province of Basilicata at Sapri.

Above: *Olive trees, many of them hundreds of years old, thrive in the region's dusty volcanic ground, their luscious green and gold oil as carefully labelled as the finest wines.*

Flora and Fauna

The geography and vegetation of this warm world is attractive as a habitat to many birds and animals. **Lizards** and insects proliferate in the heat. The balmy climate and plenty of sunshine means **exotic plants**. Everywhere ancient **olive trees** cling to the soil, roots clambering over dry rocks, and although some of the trees are extremely old they still produce a much valued olive crop. It is certainly worth bringing a bottle back.

Beyond the industrial fringes and developed areas there is a great deal of wildlife, for this is a province dominated by plenty of open space. Hills were once heavily wooded, but became denuded as wood was used for industry and building. A programme of re-planting has resulted in a return of trees over up to 25 per cent of the area. Although some plants here are imported species, (the Australian eucalyptus, for example) there are many original plants.

Tree species found here include **pines**, **beeches**, **almond** and **citrus**, with many luxuriant **shrubs** from arbutus and juniper to acanthus and myrtle.

As with any countryside pursuit, you may need to bide your time and remain quiet in order to see local fauna. They include **foxes**, **rabbits**, **squirrels** and even **wild boar**. You will be lucky indeed to see the shy and

---

BIRDS IN CAGES

Even in town centres you will hear and see bird life. Birds are popular **pets**, bred or captured, and are often seen (and heard) from their cages or on balconies. All over Italy small birds are also often used for **food**. Don't be sur-prised if you see skewered larks and thrushes on sale in the markets, or are offered them in restaurants, some-times straddled over polenta as a local delicacy.

rare **wildcat** and even shyer **wolf**, that still lurk in high and deserted mountain areas.

Many visitors only see the city and the coast, where **bird** life may be limited to doves, sparrows, or nimble swallows and the acrobatic

Above: *Visitors to Naples and the coast, will be sure to see the many doves that inhabit the region.*

swifts soaring over the rooftops of Naples. As the evening progresses small bats emerge to flitter over the towns. Among the many birds, look for hawks, owls and along the coast and in the country, numerous warblers and finches. Stars among singing birds are blue rock thrushes and nightingales.

Bird watchers might consider a trip to the north, just across the border into Lazio. Here is the **Parco Nazionale dei Circeo**. Named after the witch Circe, and the legend of Ulysses and his men turned into pigs, there are many water birds here. It is a coastal strip of a series of marshes and wetlands near Anzio, together with a large lake, the **lago di Sabaudia**.

On city approaches and along highways you will see roadside plant shops. Like all Italians, Neopolitans love to load their gardens and terraces with blooming plants, vines, shrubs, even trees. Aside from many unusual sun-loving flowers and vines, you will also see on sale a vast variety of often beautiful terra cotta pots to plant them in, as well as sentimental sculptures. These are often at bargain prices, but if tempted to buy, remember they are heavy to transport home.

Italians are still fond of using fur for garments, and aside from being expensive they can also be high fashion, so don't be too surprised if you see women draped in furs, sometimes from exotic species. (Men too may sport fur collars or hats.)

SHOOTING AWAY

Hunting is a popular Italian sport and the Neopolitans are as fond of it as anyone. There are seasons for shooting **wild game**, but it is such a passion, that you will see hunters at almost any time of year. Consequently, there is a constant searching of field and wood for almost every kind of wild animal. Some are large game, but some are very small, such as **songbirds**, It has unkindly been remarked that some sportsmen will even take aim at a butterfly.

HISTORICAL CALENDAR		
Before 1000BC Settlers live in the hills and many of the caves.	**1194–1269** Hohenstaufen Dynasty rules.	**1943** The Germans expelled from Naples.
600BC Greeks from Cumae found Neapolis.	**AD1266–1422** Naples becomes part of Angevin kingdom, under Charles I.	**1944** Another major eruption of Mount Vesuvius.
146BC Rome dominates for the next 500 years.	**1269** King Conradin beheaded.	**1950–60s** The *Cassa per il Mezzogiorno* scheme to protect historic old town.
AD79 Major eruption of Vesuvius which causes the destruction of Roman cities near the volcano.	**1443** Alfonso I of Aragon enters, Naples colony of Spain for next 300 years.	**1870s** Outbreak of cholera.
AD400 Slow establishment of the new Christian religion.	**1631** Vesuvius erupts.	**1980** Further eruptions of Mount Vesuvius.
AD555–600 Byzantine rule	**1656** The plague kills thousands of people.	**1987** Naples wins the football championship.
AD763 Naples becomes independent duchy.	**1734** Arrival of Charles of Bourbon.	**1993** Antonio Bassalino elected as mayor.
1139–1194 Normans rule	**1860** Unification of Italy. **1922** Fascists in Italy	**1994** The G7 Summit opens in July in the city.

HISTORY IN BRIEF

With its many attractive aspects the area was a favoured place to settle even in pre-recorded times. Hunters and gatherers were probably attracted by its natural geography – an easily accessible and extensive coastline with islands, and a defendable interior of hills and valleys. From ancient times it was home to Mediterranean peoples and pre-history offers a rich panoply of occupation.

Below: *One of the many quaint fishing villages to be found in the Sorrento area.*

Later, in a kind of ancient ribbon development, the coast received many settlers in antiquity, the shore becoming populated with small fishing and trading ports, settlements, religious buildings and villas. Up in the hills, small valley farms and the then vast woodlands provided a living for a tough hard-living peasant stock.

The natural beauty of the place was probably the last thing that drew

The **southern part** of the Italian peninsula was an integral part of the ancient Greek world. Long before the Romans, the Greeks had spread out from the mother country and explored their inland sea. They **colonized Sicily** and in **Campania**, the coastal towns of **Paestum**, **Cuma** and **Pozzuoli** are but three of many settlements of Greek origin. Greek colonization affected much of this coastline and early towns were used as **trading links** establishing a policy of creating settlements over much of the Mediterranean world.

Below: *Continue along the Amalfi Coast to the village of Atrani. Wedged between two cliffs and overlooking the sea, it is a favourite spot for the locals living here.*

original settlers. It was easy to get to by – water offered riches, fertile land and there was also the sea's produce. In ancient times **Greece** and **Carthage** vied for power in the enclosed world of the Mediterranean. The first recorded arrivals were the Greeks, and those curious and very civilized people who spread down from the North and Tuscany, the Etruscans. They have all left their marks. The explorers settled around Sicily and all along the Southern Italian coast, founding trading posts and harbours. Examples of their fine and impressive architecture can still be seen. They put down roots, and it is often said that Neapolitans today still have a dark, Greekish look. Indeed Greek was the common language until the end of the Roman Empire.

Rivals for power, Greece and Macedonia were finally overpowered and subjected to Rome in 146BC. Rome from then on dominated ancient Campania for more than five centuries, bringing a new life to the area. Even 2000 years ago the balmy climate meant that this area was a lure for settlers and even early tourists. Towns along the sea were usually ports, but some seem to have been special places built in particularly attractive spots for relaxation and pleasure. Certainly after detailed excavation, social life in Pompeii was revealed as being on a grand scale with a huge arena for entertainment.

Many inhabitants owned numerous luxuries in their houses and gardens, placed closely together along the narrow streets.

In the early Roman period several emperors, from **Tiberius** to **Nero**, attached themselves to Naples and its countryside. These two emperors were particularly renowned for their cruelty and venality, and Tiberius so enjoyed Capri life he actually governed the empire from there at the end of his life. Augustus lived in Ischia, later moving to Capri where his villa can be seen. Courts followed the emperors, Roman aristocrats built fine villas and well planned towns. As a rich and productive coastal region and part of the Mediterranean offering an alluring life, Campania has attracted many important settlers over the centuries.

MAJESTIC MONARCHS

The principal rulers of the royal days of Naples are depicted in **niches** in the great palace in the centre of Naples. In actual fact, these niches were created by the need to shore up the palace which was foundering due to the many underground passages and caves below the city. The architect cleverly filled alternate spaces with supporting brickwork and stood **statues** in them. It is said they tell a story in a very Neapolitan style. Their grimaces and gesticulations, supposedly point to the fact that one king has commited a *faux pas.*

Above *The gardens at the Caserta Royal Palace are famous for their ornamented pools and fountains, but the highlight has to be the spectacular waterfall, the Grande Cascata, also known as the Fountain of Diana.*

Like much of the rest of Europe the medieval period was a time of consolidation and the gradual ascendancy of the Christian church. After the first millenium passed, the desirability of attaching this beautiful part of the world to their possessions attracted the leaders of other European countries. Foreign forces have always played a continuous part in the forming of Campania, particularly the French. After the Normans penetrated from the north and set up aristocratic courts in Sicily, as well as Naples, they made their main base at the preferred Palermo. By 1302, within 40 years of Charles of Anjou becoming King of Sicily, the **Angevins** had established a court in Naples. Their domain became known as, '**The Kingdom of the Two Sicilies**'

Several aristocratic families have held sway here after the early incursions of the **Normans** from France. First the Hohenstaufens, then the Angevins (from Anjou), the Arogonese, the Spanish and eventually the French again, both Bourbons and Murats. During the 16th century, both Spain and France struggled for European domination, and for an extended time the French ruled in Campania. First the **Bourbons** ruled, but were later deposed after the Revolution and replaced by Napoleon's family, the **Murats** (who promoted good government).

During the 18th century, elegance flowered and the affluence of the aristocracy under the Bourbon family resulted in a good deal of building. Most evident is the

---

SIREN CALL

The origins of the city are very ancient. The name of **Naples** comes from the first Greek settlement of Neapolis, but the city is also associated with legend of the exotic siren, **Parthenope**. The legend claims that Naples was founded by Parthenope, who having failed to lure **Odysseus** onto the rocks of the **Li Galli Islands** off the Amalfi Coast, was herself washed up on the bay shore.

royal palace at Caserta, up in the cool hills to the north of Naples. Caserta was designed to puff up the importance of the French style and taste, but Naples itself benefited enormously from the domination of the ruling family. The royal palace and the vast San Carlo Opera House in Naples, as well as many churches, are the monuments the era has left for us to enjoy. As the turbulent 18th century faded, the resilient Bourbons were re-instated after 1815. Indeed the family survived the upheavals of revolts to continue here until 1860. The final flowering of the old rule was artistic encouragement during the neo-classical era when the fine open Piazza del Plebiscito was created. The grand square with its classical colonnade before a church was modelled on Rome's Pantheon. It has now been cleared of parked cars and can be seen as a glorious public space once again, although it seems more suited to the approach of a government hall than a church.

Royal rule was finally severed after 1860 with the arrival of **Garibaldi's armies**. Intent on the unification of Italy and the joining together of the widely differing North and the South, the general was greeted as a saviour. Intent on pulling the Italian 'boot' right up to the Alps, and the establishment of a republic for the whole of the country, the Red Shirts swept up from the south. For the first time since the Romans, Italy was a complete country and not a series of separated states.

> **SIR WILLIAM HAMILTON'S FINDS**
>
> A devotee of classical antiquity, **Sir William Hamilton** arrived in Naples in the late 18th century with his famous wife, Emma, who met Admiral Horatio Nelson here. Hamilton organized and financed several successful **excavations** around this time. There were many important finds, and Hamilton's people unearthed hundreds of artefacts at ancient sites, from **jewellery** to **armour**, and magnificent **kraters**, to **sculptures** and **vases**. Many can be seen in the fabulous collection in the Museum of Archaeology in Naples, others are displayed in the British Museum.

Below: *Restaurants and cafés line the quay at the Borgo Marinaro.*

When the **Revolution** rocked France, beheaded its Bourbon king and many aristocrats, scaring much of Europe, Naples had particular reason to fear reprisal. The city was governed by a branch of the **Bourbon family** and received emigrants such as the daughters of Louis XV. The Revolution brought a new government to Paris, and soon French troops arrived in Naples. In honour of the name Parthenope, the revolutionary (and classically minded) French set up a **Parthenopaean Republic** until Napoleon's brother became king in 1806.

After the hail of events that accompanied the unification of Italy during the 1860s, Naples and its satellite towns began to suffer a series of economic hardships. The poor countryside and signs of depression still lingering today reflect the fact that Naples had a very definite boom and bust period – one from which it has only recently begun to emerge. After the establishment of the new complete Italy, the power of the one time rich city-state dwindled. Naples now had to compete with other Italian cities, and the population (particularly of its small towns) shrivelled as the agricultural economy no longer flourished. A deep, slow economical depression began.

Naples had been strong and powerful as a self controlling unit but during the remainder of the 19th century and into the next, many problems appeared. The industrial base that had been built up was soon forfeited to the wealthy North, with its easier access to the rest of Europe. An economic slide began, resulting in poverty and eventually a crime ridden town. You can see how the failing economy affected country towns when you tour the area. Many are ghosts of what they once were, reached by badly maintained roads and with antiquated buildings. This 'unspoilt state' can be a big bonus for tourism of course, for the towns, often clustered around a castle or a cathedral, can be very appealing. Dependent still on the countryside and small businesses, they can offer simple charm.

Rather like the south of France, the coast here has always attracted **luxury lovers** and there are many **opulent seaside villas** by the shore and inland. They have been built here for over 2000 years, for the ancient (and rich) Romans enjoyed these **warm sea airs** and **scenic splendours** as much as we do today. Many of their seaside villas, often now fully excavated, are open to view, reflecting a very comfortable life. Some of these coastal places were actually holiday and retirement settlements 2000 years ago!

GOVERNMENT AND ECONOMY

There are five administrative districts within the relatively small province of Campania, the City of Naples being one of them. Each has its own administration and district seat for the elected body under a mayor, and each has, incidentally, its own tourist board.

Above: *The Italian national flag.*
Opposite: *Villa Vesuvius, situated on the clifftop in Salerno offers superb views of the Bay of Naples.*

Naples is governed by a mayor and council. They sit in the imposing Palazzo di S. Giacomo on the Municipio Square, facing the sea and the main rail station. Other government offices are in the neighbouring squares of the Plebiscito, Trente and Trieste. It has to be said that although diminished, crime still has a hand in the politics of the area. This is a city that does things its own way.

In 1993 a new mayor, Antonio Bassolino, brought much needed changes to the city, and instituted a programme to end the hold organised crime has long had here. (A similar and parallel development occurred in that other crime ridden city of the south, Palermo, under a new mayor.) This clean up of crime and domination by a few 'families' was aimed at parts of the city under the heel of the infamous Camorra. In a large new programme to support a surge of local pride, the new city administration pushed for the widespread restoration of its great palaces, museums and churches to underline the importance of the Neapolitan culture.

There has been much to do. The city of Naples developed enormously in the 20th century, particularly in the 1950s and 60s. The bombings of World War II (1939–43) resulted in much rebuilding. Although Vesuvius experiences many minor tremors, the big eruption of the volcano in 1980 stalled developments.

The principal airport is the big international Capodichino terminal at Naples. Transport is good, although some roads are poor beyond the sea shore connections, as so much of the province is mountainous.

FLOATING AROUND

It is always an adventure to **go by water** to an Italian town. Be it Venice or villages lining the lakes, you have lots of choice here. On the **Bay of Naples** you can take a variety of craft to hop along the coasts and between the islands. In high summer the sea and harbours are busy with **ferryboats**, **hydrofoils**, **private yachts** and **cruisers**. In addition cruise liners call at Naples and pause at **Capri**, **Ischia** and **Prócida**. The islands and towns such as **Sorrento** are all served by frequent and fast water services, easily reached by year-round ferry from Naples.

THE PEOPLE

The people of Naples and Catania are definitely southern in style and looks. They tend to be short, solid, dark and full of vitality. They are described as vivacious and vital, yet they live in a world of fantasy and superstition, not to say magic, rendering them at times mournful and fatalistic.

As soon as you leave Rome behind, you enter the warm south, and a very different feeling is obvious on the narrow streets of Naples and its satellite towns. Crowded and noisy with chaotic traffic, the capital is like no other Italian city. Although the province and Naples have had a long and difficult 100 year decline, the forces that are changing the city are bringing in new business and it is enlivening and enriching a town that was once in a wretched state. Although much of Naples still seems decrepit and dirty, the changes are far reaching, and the effects ongoing.

It is a society that takes advantage of the climate and loves the outdoors, be it street life in a city or sitting beside a square and enjoying life as it goes by in a small town. At ease and at work, they enjoy and share a theatricality that is nationally recognized. Neapolitans use their voices in song, that's very true, but they are also born actors and mimics. Displayed in public spaces, in squares, churches and parks you can see a regular expression of this exuberant art, for which Neapolitans

Right: *Graffiti is an ancient Neapolitan art-form, proudly displayed at Pompeii and, in updated form, in central Naples.*

are justly famed. They use the voice all the time, some-times flaring into passion, but add a language that is universal – that of the body. Feet, hands, fingers, heads, arms, shoulders, torsos are all employed, and used to great dramatic advantage here as people converse volubly, both vocally and physically.

Above: To be young and cool in Naples requires three things – black sun-glasses, a leather jacket and a moped.

Sport and Recreation

You have plenty of opportunity here to see a range of sporting activities. There is **golf**, **tennis**, **horse racing** and plenty of unusual things too. Becoming a popular local sport is a fast and exciting ballgame. Known as *peyote* in South America, it uses the long handled stick with a basket for hurling a ball.

Of the spectator sports **football**, or *calcio*, as in so many Italian cities, is a real passion, its star players raised to the elevation of gods. Matches are attended by huge crowds. Not always a position to be envied as it is a career that often ends very early. You go up – and you come down. The biggest name here in Naples is probably the star player **Maradona**, who rose to a meteoric height in local adoration, and even had a pizza created for him at the height of his fame in the likeness of his large-eared face. Eventually he fell into a sad world of obesity and unsavoury habits after a sad decline.

FOLK EVENTS

Song and **Dance** are impor-tant here and there are many local festivities, even festivals. Often you can join in. The showy Neapolitan **costumes** are an integral part of the popular art, and even if you don't see actual presentations you can't avoid the strident, infectious and often senti-mental **music**. It echoes out everywhere, from solitary players, strolling **bands** and **radio** programmes, adding to the gaiety of the place.

Above: *Neapolitans, like most Italians are known for their style and sense of fashion. There are many clothing stores in Naples, but if you are looking for an upmarket boutique, try Via Chiaia.*

SOUVENIRS

There is no lack of souvenirs to be found here, and local people are industrious and ingenious at making all sorts of things for sale. The Neapolitans have a fanciful imagination and it is challenged by anything clever or amusing. On the streets you will see many small stalls set up to sell **embroideries**, **trinkets** and **figurines**. Browse, but best perhaps to check in local shops. Look for good souvenirs in the **museums**, and **palace shops** such as at Capodimonte and Caserta, or Portici, another Bourbon residence.

Campania has been catering to tourists for many centuries, providing them with a range of services, pleasures and things to do and see. The **shopping** here is now as intriguing as any large Italian city with a range of well designed clothes, table ware, ornaments, artefacts and art objects. In turn, the flow of money has been welcomed, and now that Naples has turned a corner and is losing its dark image of dirt and crime it should be alluring to even more visitors. Among useful pastimes in the region are the making and display of souvenirs. The famous cribs and carved figures are only one aspect of the souvenir business.

A major slice of the people in Campania is not composed of residents. Inevitably Naples and its beautiful coasts are an attraction to many Italians as well as foreign visitors. It is a burden that local people have to bear that most visitors will arrive by road, for not only Neapolitans love their **cars**. Every weekend, most especially in summer, the roads south from Rome are filled with cars heading to the beaches and bars of the many resorts here. Naples is certainly a grubby city in many of its aspects and neighbourhoods, but it could well do without the exhaust fumes of summer visitors. A world problem of course, as in the affluent countries or Europe, inhabitants love to use their vehicles.

The Arts

Naples is a theatrical city, renowned throughout Italy for its flamboyance. Small wonder that **dance**, **music** and **mime** are appreciated in settings that are often theatre sets themselves. Scaramouch, the foxy old man of the **Commedia dell'Arte**, was born here. Music, dance and opera are popular here and you will find street singers and entertainers of many kinds. Italy is ever a musical country, and Naples particularly so. Its mellifluous, sentimental songs are very popular.

In a city where life seems a theatrical art there are many **theatres** and **cinemas**. One of the biggest **opera houses** in Italy is here in Naples. Built in 1737, remodelled in 1816, the Teatro San Carlo is among the most famous of all the places of entertainment in Italy. It is a truly regal opera house. It is unprepossessing outside, standing beside the Palazzo Reale and the monumental arcades of the Galleria Umberto. Within it is a different tale. This is a classic Italian house with five levels of boxes surrounding a pit before the stage, built as much for social pleasures as for art.

CLASSIC POP SONG

One of the best known Neapolitan songs (and there are many of them) is the famous **Funiculee**, **Funicula**. This was a song that found its inspiration in an odd source – the popularity of a new **railway** built to ascend the slopes of the volcano. It's still heard but alas; the old mountain funicular no longer functions. You will, however, find four hill climbing rail links right in Naples itself.

Below: *The magnifcent interior of the Teatro San Carlo. The lavish red-and-gold concert hall can seat around 3000 people, and is known for its brilliant accoustics.*

There is a regular opera and ballet season here, with visits from foreign companies too, and you can tour the theatre at certain times when it is not in performance or being used for rehearsals.

Undoubtedly one of the greatest attractions here is the vast **Museum of Archaeology** on the northern edge of the central city. Here many of the most important finds from the classical sites around the city are to be found. Even if you are not intrigued with Roman and Greek history, you must not miss this museum. Housed in a 16th-century building are galleries of sculpture (Roman and Greek), mosaics and frescoes (many from Herculaneum and Pompeii) as well as numerous small bronzes, silver, ivory and glass along with simple kitchen utensils. Together they make up one of the most important museums in the world for Greek and Roman arts. There is also a gallery with items depicting the history of Naples.

Below: *The Farnese Hercules at the Museo Archeologico Nazionale.*

Unfortunately galleries can often be closed, so you may need to plan to visit this fascinating place again.

There are museums at the **Certosa di San Martino**, showing the famous 18th-and 19th-century Neapolitan cribs and figurines. And at the **Capodimonte Palace** the Pinacoteca holds some fine works from **Bellini** to **Correggio**, as well as works from outside Italy, including two rare **Breughels**. Also here are the Royal apartments with a display of porcelain. At the **Palazzo Como** are ceramics, arms and armour and a collection of paintings, housed in a handsome rusticated palace. There is a carriage museum at the **Museo Principe di Aragona**.

The Visual Arts

Early visitors were **Giotto**, **Simone Martini** and sculptors, some brought by **King Robert of Anjou**, who also drew Petrarch and Boccaccio to his city. There is a particular school of Neapolitan painting that flourished in the 17th and up to the 18th century, a vibrant time, whose main figure is the master **Caravaggio**. His followers include **Luca Giordano** and **Carraciolo**. You can see examples of this period at the city's galleries and in churches.

Above: *The statue of Charles III, by Antonio Canova, in the Piazza del Plebiscito.*

Unlike some other Italian provinces, however, you will not find many major artists in Campania. Rather there is a plethora of extraordinary decoration, particularly in the countryside with florid pictures and clever effects, anonymous sculptures in towns and in the churches, carved by local artisans who are often inventive craftsmen.

While the architecture of the city is unusual it is not unique in style. Yet many fine artists have worked here – **Fernando Sanfelice** was an architect with flamboyant tastes who created elegant courtyards with his trademark staircases as stellar features. **Luigi Vanvitelli** designed the Royal palace, and later the palace of Caserta. He was also a sculptor, while the great **Canova** carved statues (two are on the central Piazza Plebiscito). When you go into local churches, however, you will find plenty to look at – mostly exuberant local works, colourful yet more in the style of folk art.

> **ANTIQUE CONNOISSEUR**
>
> Just to show that museums are not modern inventions, look at the the first floor gallery of the **Museo Archeologico** for the rooms dedicated to the **Villa di Pisone**, buried at Herculaeum. It probably belonged to a collector, who may have been related to **Julius Caesar**. In antiquity this was a private collection of extraordinary objects. They range from a series of statues to the priceless contents of a library of papyrus sheets.

Architecture

Naples has amazing buildings, none more extraordinary than a parade of high Baroque monuments that reach the heights of both interior and exterior decoration, very-much to the gaudy Neapolitan taste. There are literally dozens of palaces and churches in the

Above: *The ornate Baroque interior of the Church of Gesù Nuovo. The church is situated in the long street, also known as Spaccanapoli.*

crowded streets and squares, the ornaments of this once splendid and affluent city. At last, after many decades of decay, these often over-the-top, yet splendid buildings are beginning to be cared for. If you are only able to visit one, make it the **Church of Gesù Nuovo** which was once a palace fronted with diamond-faced stones. (It is similar to the Palazzo dei Diamante in Ferrara.)

In the piazza before it is a theatrical monument, a tall Baroque column to the Virgin. Just along the street is a contrast – once overlaid with Baroque decoration the tall, high church of Santa Chiara was restored to its pure Provençal Gothic style after war-time bombing in 1943. In contrast two formidable fortresses, the severe and sea girt **Castel dell'Ovo in Santa Lucia** of Norman origin and the impressive **Castel Nuovo** right in the city centre, are monumental examples of their era. The latter is also a marriage of styles, a 13th-century stronghold modelled on an example in the country of the then-rulers, far-off Anjou and the grand castle of Angers. It has an enchanting entry of sculpted white marble in the Renaissance manner. More contrasts? The main rail station squatting on the water front is an exercise in the bulky yet impressive Mussolini-esque style of the late 1930s. Beside **Art Deco** examples, Naples also has **Art Nouveau** touches.

THE ART OF NAPLES

To see examples of the famed 17th-century **'Caravaggioesque'** school in Naples, often in a style that borders dramatic excess, go to the art gallery or visit the institute of **Decumanus Maximus** and the **Pio Monte della Misericordia**. Six panels illustrate the charitable philosophy of the house, one by Caravaggio illustrates the theme of the **Seven Works of Mercy**. Carraciolo is also represented with his work, **St Peter Released From Prison**.

Food and Drink

Agriculture has always been the key facet of the area beyond Naples. Despite the fact that over 80 per cent of the province is hilly or mountainous. No doubt about it, the food and **wine** of this fertile area is abundant, lush and delicious. The fields and terraces of the country produce a great variety of **vegetables** and tree-ripened **fruits** from the rich soils and constant sun. These include oranges, lemons, tangerines, figs, nectarines, apricots, peaches and melons, while asparagus and artichokes are early arrivals. The vines laced along their terraces are loaded with grapes in season for making wine, and also for the dessert dishes of the area. A range of local **cheeses** is found in the country. Ricotta and mozarella (from the buffalo) are often used in cooking. Plenty of **meats** too; try the dried and cured meats, raw and cooked ham and sausages. There are cakes and desserts that are unique to Campania which should definitely be sampled.

From the sea come huge harvests of **fish** and **crustacea**. The shellfish is amazingly varied. Markets, on the streets of the towns, show just how much harvest the sea produces. Not surprisingly one of the businesses of Naples is food processing.

Below: *Try the ricotta and mozzarella cheeses, made from buffalo milk.*

Even if you can't take back fresh fruits and meats, they are **preserved** and **cured** in many ways here, from **sausages** to smoked **hams**. Neapolitan **salami** comes in neat packages, is spicy and well fatted. Visit a grocery or supermarket to find tinned **vegetables** and preserved meats that are vacuum wrapped. Capri specializes in bottled fruits using local **liqueurs**. You can find **berries** in fruit liqueurs, **prunes** in anise, and sometimes **nuts** too. These expensive little jars are not always a luxury you may buy for yourself, but they make good gifts.

Naples is internationally famous for two popular foodstuffs. The city has come up with at least two well-known dishes, which were first created here. One, the **pizza** was born in the back streets and can still be tasted in its original forms even in smart little restaurants. It is certainly to be found at its best here. Basically a flat pie made of tomato, cheese and additional garnishes decided by the cook, it is best baked in a brick oven, so that its special dough crisps on the hot floor, and it is still very much a local delicacy.

Even better known – and almost a symbol of Italy – is **spaghetti**. This is the local pasta form and now known around the world, available in Italian restaurants as far apart as Sydney and San Francisco. Spaghetti in long thin strands cooked to the correct *al dente* consistency then looped in deep plates, oiled or creamed, and married to a myriad sauces is definitely a Neapolitan dish. Here you can sample the authentic classic version. One of these is *con vongole*, or with little clams in their shells.

The ancient olive trees provide the deep golden oil that is the base of so many Italian dishes. You can also buy the **oil** to take home. Salad dishes are inventive and richly dressed.

Try eating **alfresco**. Lots of possibilities for picnics here – shop locally for all sorts of crusty breads, olives,

Below: *The Pugliano Market in Ercolano, one of the many fruit and vegetable markets found in Naples.*

nuts, cheeses, hams, olives and the tangy, locally produced salami. There are plenty of fresh vegetables, salads and fruits, and to drink try a local '*birra*' or **beer**, or fresh chilled white **wine** from the vineyards on the slopes of Vesuvius.

Vines have been carefully cultivated here for thousands of years, and wine of the locality was famed as long ago as the time of the Roman emperors. (Wine shops were excavated at Pompeii with sunken bowls in their stone counters as well as pottery containers). Even in this generally dulcet Mediterranean clime they are cosseted, the tender shoots protected against possible winter chills with straw and rattan matting. In the ripening season grapes cluster along long lines of vines. Some are for eating but most are used for local wine production.

The wines that come from the terraces of the mountainside are much enjoyed. The long looping vines ranging high up the mountain-side produce red wines from heavy bunches of grapes swollen from the volcanic soil they thrive in. Best know varieties are **Falerno** while Ischia produces white wines including the **Mount Epomeo** reds and whites. **Capri** has both red and white too, which can be sampled at small local inns. It is claimed that the wines of Campania benefit from a tinge of the volcanic sulphur in the subsoil in their bouquets.

Above Left: *The Neapolitans also produce delicious liqueurs. Displayed here is the sweet, yellow Strega ('witch'), which is meant to have magical powers.*

2
Naples

Naples has never been an ordinary city, but one that has lived at extremes of luxury, cruelty, poverty, beauty, indolence and fire. In its 2900 year old history, it has been ruled by the Greeks, Romans, Byzantines, Normans, Spanish, French and, only belatedly, the Italians. Largely cut off by political and geographic boundaries from northern Italy, it has looked to the sea and developed an extraordinarily cosmopolitan feel. For centuries outsiders, whether travellers or northern Italians, have described the people of Naples as being passionate, romantic and poetic or as lazy, shiftless and untrustworthy. Whatever the reality, they arouse strong feelings in the outsider; not once has anyone claimed the city or its people to be boring.

The 20th century saw Naples decline abruptly, stripped of power by the unification of Italy. As poverty and neglect swept its streets, the city fully deserved its reputation as a den of crime. However, while not yet perfect, things have improved dramatically in recent years and those who fall back on out of date clichés miss one of the most entertaining – and beautiful – cities on the Mediterranean.

Naples has an incomparable setting. Lord Byron rated it second only to Constantinople (Istanbul). Many of its buildings are crumbling, but they do so aesthetically, while others have merited from an almost miraculous grand cleanup and renovation that is gradually restoring the city to its rightful place on the European stage, with fine architecture and museums, wonderful restaurants and nightlife, and fascinating streets perfectly designed for strolling.

DON'T MISS

*** **Museo Archeologico Nazionale**: a great collection of Graeco-Roman art.
*** **Spaccanapoli**: this street is the last surviving relic of the ancient Greek grid plan.
*** **Porto di Santa Lucia**: the medieval **Castel dell' Ovo** surrounded by the Borgo Marinara (Fishermen's Quarter).
*** **Parco e Museo Nazionale di Capodimonte**: a beautiful palace, art collection and park.
** **Certosa di San Martino**: the best view out across Naples and the Bay.

Opposite: *The 19th-century Galleria Umberto I with its impressive glass-dome roof.*

NAMING FOR POSTERITY

The very first Greek settlement of Paleopolis (Old Town), built in the 8th–7th centuries BC stood on the site of Santa Lucia and the Castel dell'Ovo. In the 5th century, the city was moved to a new site, now the Centro Storico, and renamed Neapolis (New City). Over the next 2500 years, this turned into Napoli. The Greek and Roman harbour now houses the naval dockyard next to the ferry port.

Below: *The striking marble Arco di Trionfo stands out from the Castel Nuovo.*

NAPLES BY AREA

The best way to get your bearings is to look at Naples from the sea, with the city laid out in front of you like a map, each area ascending the last to reach the clifftop.

Naples is laid out along the northern section of a horseshoe bay. Along the northern arm (to your left) are the towns of **Pozzuoli**, built on a volcanic field, known as the **Campi Flegrei** (*see* page 53) and the elegant suburb of **Posillipo**. At the corner is the resort area of **Mergellina**. Beyond this, just to the left of the city centre, is the seaside walkway, the **Lungomare**, fronted by several of the city's finest hotels and definitely the place to stay. Just behind and above the Lungomare, **Chiaia**, an area first constructed by the Spanish in the 17th–18th centuries, is now one of the city's trendiest shopping and nightlife areas, filled with designer boutiques and bijou bistros.

Continuing up the cliff, the upmarket residential district of **Vomero** is wrapped around the vast **Castel Sant'Elmo**. Built mainly in the 19th century, the suburb cascades across the peak and down the far side of the ridge.

Directly below it, halfway down the cliff, and largely tucked out of sight is the **Centro Storico** (Historic Centre) – the original city centre. The area is generally considered to be bounded to the west by Via Toledo, to the north by Piazza Cavour, and to the east by Corso Garibaldi. To the south, it technically stretches down to the waterfront, but the boundary of the 'tourist' zone is marked by **Piazza Bovio** (former home of the Stock Exchange) and **Corso Umberto I**, built as a slum clearance project to connect the port and railway station in the early 20th century.

Back on the seafront, almost exactly at the centre of the bay, you come to the city's most famous marker, the 12th-century **Castel dell'Ovo** (Castle of

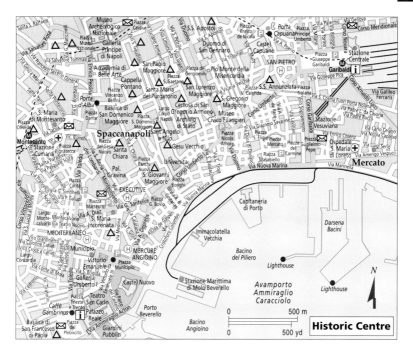

Historic Centre

the Egg), and a little peninsula on which stands the traditional fishermen's quarter of **Santa Lucia**.

Just to the right (south) of this are the city's main ferry port, and the Spanish royal city centre, dominated by the brooding bulk of the **Castel Nuovo** and the **Palazzo Reale**. The rest of the seafront is taken up by both naval and commercial dockyards. Just behind these, on Piazza Garibaldi, is the **Stazione Centrale**. The areas along this stretch of the waterfront and round the station are very rough and unsafe for walking at night.

Above them on the clifftop, the **Capodimonte** area is lush, green and peaceful, with one of the city's best museums and several good hotels. Finally, continue south and you see the towering cone of **Mount Vesuvius** (*see* page 63), totally surrounded by poorer commuter suburbs. Amongst them is **Ercolano** (*see* page 65), built on the ruins of ancient Herculaneum.

PLANNING FOR THE FUTURE

As the older areas of central Naples are swamped by a sea of ugly and often poorly constructed apartment blocks, the biggest concern facing planners is creating sufficient through routes to evacuate the huge population of the city (now over 2 million) should Vesuvius erupt again. It will take at least 10 years to put their contingency plans into effect, but the volcano is already overdue.

Above: *The Museo Archeologico Nazionale has an extensive collection of ancient art.*

SIGHTSEEING IN NAPLES

Archaeological Museum

The Museo Archeologico Nazionale is tragically and obviously short of money, and desperately needs a facelift, but inside is housed one of the world's greatest treasure troves of classical art and sculpture, the combined resources of several important collections, including finds from Herculaneum (housed here since 1797); Pompeii; and the world-famous Farnese Collection, brought to Naples when Charles III Bourbon inherited it from his mother, Elizabeth Farnese in 1731.

As you enter, the ground floor is a tranquil marble world of **Graeco-Roman sculpture** including various gods and goddesses, sportsmen, politicians and sarcophagi. Amongst them is a fascinating set of portrait busts of Socrates, Euripides and, supposedly, Homer, along with various Roman emperors, and a 2nd century AD statue of the many-breasted Artemis from Ephesus. However the highlights both come from the Caracalla Baths in Rome – a superb statue of Hercules, all curly hair and rippling muscles, and the massive Farnese Bull, a complex, towering sculpture telling the legend of Dirce, who was tied to a bull and tortured by her stepsons, Ampheon and Zethus. Beyond, stairs lead down to the basement, and a fascinating collection of **Egyptian art** sadly overlooked here amongst the jewels of Pompeii.

Head up to the mezzanine floor and turn left for a dazzling array of **Pompeii mosaics**, of which the most important undoubtedly depicts Alexander the Great's epic victory over King Darius of Persia. To most visitors however, this pales beside the more domestic charms of the *Cave Canem* (beware of the dog) sign, the fighting cocks, the marine mosaic showing an octopus and lobster locked in conflict, or the simple picture of doves drinking from a bowl.

Across the hallway, to the right, the **Napoli Antica Gallery** houses a small display of the history of Naples, together with an interesting collection of ancient household utensils and some beautifully modelled votive terracotta heads.

Up on the first floor, turn left for a stunning collection of small bronzes, silver, glass and ivory from Pompeii and Herculaneum with elaborately decorated helmets and oil lamps and the magnificent glass Blue Vase – the inspiration for centuries of Wedgewood design. A partial reconstruction of the Temple of Isis helps to put many of the finds in this section into context before you arrive at the superb collection of frescoes from Pompeii, Herculaneum, Stabia and Paestum. Many follow the familiar themes of ancient mythology, but there are also landscapes, portraits and trompe l'œil architectural studies, all still brilliantly fresh in colour and emotion.

The first room to the right of the main stairs is dedicated to the collection of the Roman antiquarian who lived in the Villa de Pisone, Herculaneum, amongst which was a priceless library of 800 parchments (photos only on display). Perhaps even more awe-inspiring in the gem collection beyond is the Farnese Cup, probably carved in Ptolemaic Alexandria, as a giant, exquisite cameo.

THE *CENTRO STORICO* (HISTORIC CENTRE)

A short distance downhill from the Archaeological Museum, **Piazza Dante** was built by Charles III on the site of an old market. Its monumental columns

> **HORSES TO COURSES**
>
> The building now housing the Archaeological Museum was originally commissioned in 1582 as the Royal Riding School, but the site proved unsuitable and a university was created here instead. Between 1701–35, it was used as barracks before being returned to the students until 1797, when it first became a museum, art school and studio, and national library. With more and more collections being added it began to bulge at the seams, and gradually various elements were moved out. By 1957, the museum had assumed its current form.

Below: *An excellent collection of frescoes have been unearthed in Pompeii.*

TOO MUCH TO SEE

Although distances are
not long, start early when
exploring the *Centro Storico*.
Not only are the churches
incredibly thick on the
ground, but most only open
in the morning. The tourist
office in Piazza del Gesù
can provide a detailed map
showing four historic walking
itineraries around the old
town, taking in most of
the churches and palazzos,
as well as the signposted
Via dell'Arte.

at the back represent the virtues of the king, but his various autocratic noses and the 18th-century elegance of his design are perpetually troubled these days by the exhaust fumes of a hundred buses. At the back of the piazza, a small tunnel lined with bookshops leads through the **Porta d'Alba**, one of the original city gates, taking you instantly into a different world of tiny, dark alleys. A block in, pretty **Piazza Bellini** has a monument to the composer, Vincenzo Bellini and a variety of attractive cafés. Nearby is an 18th-century convent which now houses a fine collection of 19th-century paintings by local artists, the **Accademia di Belle Arte** (Academy of Fine Arts; Via Vincenzo Bellini 36). The piazza marks the start of Via Tribunali, the most northerly of three main east-west thoroughfares of the ancient Greek city (Decumani). Next block down is the second road, the famous Spaccanapoli; little remains of the third ancient road, to the south. There are quite a few fascinating churches along Via Tribulani, but conserve some strength and don't try to visit them all; the entire old town is crammed with churches and several are unmissable. Those on Via Tribulani include the renaissance **Cappella Pontano**, baroque **Santa Maria del Purgatorio**, and the richly decorated baroque **San Paolo Maggiore** which stands on the site of the ancient forum, next to one of the entrances to underground Naples (*see* page 44); and the magnificent medieval **San Lorenzo Maggiore**, built in 1265, although the interior is a feast of baroque excess. It is here that Boccaccio is said to have first seen his muse, Fiammetta, while Petrarch lived next door. The cloister gives access to various archaeological excavations including the

Roman macellum (market place). Last stop on the street is the **Pio Monte della Misericordia**, a 17th-century charitable institution for the poor and ill Christian slaves freed from the Ottomans. Amongst several fine paintings is an altarpiece by Caravaggio depicting *The Seven Works of Mercy*.

At the far end of the road, turn left for the **Duomo di San Gennaro** (Cathedral of St Jannarius; Via Duomo 147), consecrated in 1315, but considerably altered over the years – the Gothic façade actually belongs to the late 19th century. The building is not one of the finest

in the city, but there are several interesting points, including the **Cappella del Tesoro di San Gennaro**, home to the two miraculous phials of the blood of San Gennaro, patron saint of Naples; frescoes by Luca Giordano; an intricate 17th-century gilded wood ceiling; a 5th-century **Baptistry** and the early Christian basilica, **Santa Restituta**. The monumental spire in Piazza Riario Sforza, the **Guglia di San Gennaro** was erected to thank San Gennaro for saving Naples from the eruption of 1631. A couple of blocks down Via Duomo is a fine building that has done duty as a late 15th-century palace and 16th-century monastery and is now the **Museo Civico Filangieri** (Filangieri Museum; Via Duomo), home to the fine art collection of Prince Gaetano Filangieri.

Return to the Via Tribulani and turn left beside San Lorenzo Maggiore onto **Via San Gregorio Armeno**, Clustered along this little sidestreet are the workshops of many makers of *presepi* (Christmas cribs). The crafting of *presepi* is traditionally a family affair, with workshops handed down through the generations. Look very closely at the detail. At the centre you will find the Holy Family, but in addition to the traditional shepherds

Above: *Most Neapolitans are religious, demonstrated in the many wall shrines.*
Opposite: *Stop for lunch at a sunny pavement café at Piazza Bellini.*

MIRACLE BLOOD

In AD305, under the reign of Diocletian, San Gennaro (St Januarius), the Bishop of Benevento, was martyred and taken to the catacombs of Naples for burial. En route, his blood liquified in the hands of St Severus, who had the foresight to save two phials. Since then, twice a year, in May and September, the miracle is repeated amidst great celebration. It is taken as an omen of good fortune for the city and the occasional no-show is greeted with prophesies of disaster.

and wise men, you will find hundreds of other characters, from Turks to crippled beggars, musicians and the aristocracy.

Just off the road, is the **Certosa di San Gregorio Armeno** (Monastery of St Gregory of Armenia), a convent founded in the 8th century by a group of nuns who fled the Iconoclasts in Byzantium to preserve the relics of St Gregory. Rebuilt in the 15th and 16th centuries with an elegant cloister, today, the interior is sumptuously decorated with a 16th-century gilded wood ceiling, two Baroque organs, and 18th-century frescoes by Luca Giordano.

BUILDING THE NATIVITY

The *presepio* (Christmas crib) is one of Naples' most enduring art forms, first mentioned in 1025. Originally simple, they began to grow in scale and complexity from the 16th century onwards. The size of the scene is immaterial, from elaborate creations as large as a small room, depicting entire towns, to exquisite miniatures housed in an eggshell. Most are made of terracotta, but there are versions in wood, papier maché, plaster and even coral. The whole scene must be one not only of plenty, but severe over-indulgence, laden with tiny hams, pasta, cheese, bread, fruit and cakes. Today, people are again beginning to create modern dress figurines.

SPACCANAPOLI

Continue along Via San Gregorio Armeno and turn left onto Via San Biagio dei Librai, a treasure trove of antiques and handicrafts and the first stage on your tour of the famous Spaccanapoli. If it is open, make a quick stop at the impressively decorated Cappella dei Monte di Pietà, in the Palazzo Carafa, a charitable foundation built in 1597–1605 with a magnificent 18th-century sacristy. The entrance is flanked by sculptures by Pietro Bernini (1601).

As you continue down the street, look to your right for the **Largo Corpo di Napoli** (Body of Naples), an ancient Greek statue that has been adopted as one of the symbols of the city (*see* panel, page 39). On the other side of the road, the 15th-century **Church of Sant'Angelo a Nilo**, has a magnificent tomb sculpted by Donatello in 1426 and shipped down from Pisa. Its inhabitant is Cardinal Rinaldo Brancaccio, founder of the church, whose family palace stood next door.

The window-shopping gets better and better as Spaccanapoli becomes more trendy and affluent. The **Piazza San Domenico Maggiore** has one of the most stylish cafés in the city, ideal for a break before delving back into the churches and the **Basilica di San Domenico Maggiore**. Originally built in 1238, there is little sign of its medieval origins in either its 16th-century exterior or 19th-century neo-Gothic interior. However, there are 45 Aragonese tombs, some 14th-century frescoes, probably by Pietro Cavallini, a pupil of Giotto, and a supposedly miraculous crucifix, which is said to have spoken to St Thomas Aquinas, who lived nearby. It can be found in the Capellone del Crocifisso.

Just behind the church, an alley on the right leads to one of the highlights of the old city, the charming little **Cappella Sansevero** (Sansevero Chapel; Via de Sancti) built as the Sangro family funeral chapel in 1590. It has

MOTHER OF THE CITY

One of Naples' most cherished symbols is a small Hellenistic statue of a reclining man that represents the God of the Nile. The gender confusion began when it was discovered, headless, in the Middle Ages and those trying to decipher its meaning interpreted the cherubs (tributaries of the Nile) as suckling at the breast of the Mother-City. The head, complete with a full, bushy beard, was only finally found and restored in the 17th century, but it is still sometimes known as the 'Mother of the City'.

Opposite: *Long, straight Spaccanapoli cuts through the heart of old Naples, and contains some fantastic churches and palazzos.*
Left: *The Piazza Gesù Nuovo is the main square in the old city.*

THE GREAT DIVIDE

The Spaccanapoli is the most famous street in Naples, but you will never find its name (meaning 'Naples-splitter') on a map. The ramrod straight thoroughfare that bisects the old city is known by various names along its length. It is one of the few surviving remnants of the original ancient Greek city. Parts of the old Greek city walls have been excavated in Piazza Bellini, on the edge of the old town.

some fine frescoes and paintings, but these are outshone by three superb sculptures – *Chastity* (a veiled woman) and *Despair* (a man struggling with a net), to either side of the altar, and the extraordinary *Veiled Christ* by Guiseppe Sammartino in the centre. Prince Raimondo de Sangro, responsible for remodelling the chapel in 1749–71, was a legendary character who dabbled in alchemy, sorcery and science. In the crypt are two of his anatomical models – strange skeletons with 'petrified' veins.

Back on Spaccanapoli, now called Via B. Croce, is the freestanding belfry of **Santa Chiara**. The entrance to the Poor Clare convent built in 1310–28 by Sancia de Mallorca, wife of King Robert the Wise is just around the corner on Via Benedetto Croce. Astonishingly plain and simple inside (the result of bomb damage in 1943), it does have several fine tombs including those of Robert the Wise (1343), by Florentine sculptors Giovanni and Pacio Bertini, and Marie de Valois. The real highlight however is the beautiful Gothic cloister, reached by a separate entrance on Via Santa Chiara. In 1742, Domenico Antonio Vaccaro covered the pillars and walls in a series of fabulous majolica tiles which bring a smile to the lips and peace to the soul – a far, light-hearted cry

Below: *The magnificent gothic cloisters of the Santa Chiara are covered in beautiful majolica tiles.*

from most excessive church decoration of the period. Beside the cloister is a small museum housing various church treasures.

Beyond Santa Chiara, you reach the **Piazza del Gesù Nuovo** (New Jesus Square), the main square of the old city and home to the city tourist office.

The egg-box style stone studding of the **Church of Gesù Nuovo** (New Church of Jesus) was originally intended to be part of the Palazzo Sanseverino, but it remained unfinished and in 1584, the Jesuits converted the building into an overblown homage to baroque indulgence, every surface patterned, decorated and/or gilded. In keeping with the theme, the 19th-century altar is inlaid with semi-precious stones. The huge marble **Guglia dell'Immacolata** (Spire of Mary Immaculata), situated in the centre of the square was erected by the Jesuits in 1743.

From here, go to **Via Toledo** – lined with boutiques, it is one of the most famous shopping streets in Naples. It was named after the Viceroy who demolished the city walls to build it in 1536, and leads down towards royal Naples.

Above: *The Castel dell'Ovo is the oldest castle in Naples, and stands over the city as if to protect it.*

ROYAL NAPLES

Down on the seafront, near the main passenger port, the Art Deco **Stazione Marittima di Molo Beverello**, built in 1936, is at the heart of royal Naples. The formidable, crenellated **Castel Nuovo** (New Castle; Piazza Municipio), also known as Maschio Angioino (Angevin Keep) was built by the Angevins in 1279, in place of two earlier royal residences, the Castel dell'Ovo *(see page 44)* and the Castello di Capuano, now the city law courts, near the Porta di Capuana. Following a grand

(see page 44)

> **IF ONLY...**
>
> *The museum is full, as you know of lovely Greek bronzes. The only bother is that they all walk about the town at night.*
>   Oscar Wilde, Letter to Ernest Dowson, 11 October 1897.

Above: *Construction for the Palazzo Reale began in 1600 under Viceroy Fernández Ruiz de Castro, but was only completed in 1843. Visit the Royal Apartments to get a feel for Bourbon splendour.*

RENAISSANCE KING

Much that is finest and most beautiful in Naples was the inspiration of Bourbon King Charles III, son of Philip V of Spain and Elisabeth Farnese, who installed himself on the throne in 1734. Amongst his other achievements, he built the San Carlos Opera House, the Palazzo Capodimonte (to house the superb Farnese art collection that he inherited from his mother), and was responsible for starting the excavation of Pompeii.

---

tradition of naming, this 'new' castle is now one of the oldest buildings in Naples, built originally by the Angevins in 1279. The basic shape remains that of a classic Norman castle, but the interior was heavily altered in 1443. The castle's chief asset is a magnificent 15th-century gateway, the **Arco di Trionfo di Alfonso**, designed by Francesco Laurana in 1467 to celebrate the life and achievements of the Aragonese king, Alfonso il Magnanimo (the Magnanimous). Inside, have a look at the view from the top floors, the rib-vaulted ceiling of the **Sala dei Baroni** (Barons' Hall), now the city Council Chamber, the **Museo Civico** (City Museum), and the 13th-century **Cappella Palatina** (Palatine Chapel), which tells the story of Naples through a series of 14th–19th century paintings, sculptures and *objects d'art*.

Next to the **Castel Nuovo**, the vast dark reddish building is the **Palazzo Reale** (Royal Palace; Piazza del Plebiscito 1), built by the Spanish Viceroy in 1600, in preparation for a state visit by Philip III (which was later cancelled). Successions of Viceroys lived here in high style until 1743, when Charles III eventually moved in. Each newly arrived dynasty wished to stamp their mark on the palace and work continued up until 1843. Thirty of the State Apartments are on display, reached via an imposing double staircase. Most are richly ornamented and furnished, often in a rather cumbersome Spanish Imperial style, but two stand out above the crowd, the

King's delightful little private theatre, the **Teatrino di Cort**, and the lavishly decorated 19th-century **Cappella Reale** (Royal Chapel).

The **Ala delle Feste Wing** of the palace now houses one of Italy's most important historic libraries, the **Biblioteca Nazionale** (National Library; guided visits only). Amongst its treasures are several parchments rescued from Herculaneum and some magnificently illustrated medieval manuscripts. The **Stables** are used for temporary exhibitions.

Beyond the palace stretches the huge, pedestrianized parade ground of the **Piazza del Plebiscito**, laid out by Joachim Murat in 1810 as a place for processions and festivals. On the far side, the neo-classical Basilica di San Francesco di Paola is a close copy of the Pantheon in Rome, designed by Pietro Bianchi in 1817 to celebrate King Ferdinand's return to the throne.

Before leaving the piazza, stop at one of the city's oldest and most glamorous cafés, the **Caffè Gambrinus**, dating from 1860 and the literary haunt of visitors from Guy de Maupassant to Oscar Wilde. It is a charming way to while away an hour sampling delicious coffee and cake amongst the Belle Epoque paintings and smart Neapolitan ladies in hats and gloves.

Below: *Caffè Gambrinus (Via Chiaia), founded in 1860, is one of the oldest and most popular cafés in Naples.*

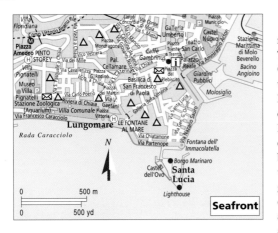

On one side of the next pretty little **Piazza Trieste e Trento** is the **Galleria Umberto I**. It was designed in 1887 by Emanuele Rocco as part of the Urban Renewal Plan following the cholera epidemic of 1884. The building is breathtaking, with elaborately decorated galleries, a glass and iron dome by Paolo Boubée as delicate and intricate as a spider's web and patterned marble pavements, but is currently in an inexplicable commercial slump.

On the other side the **Teatro San Carlo**, Italy's oldest opera house, was first built in 1737, then rebuilt after a fire in 1816. The sumptuous interior symphony of red and gold, with 184 boxes arranged in seven tiers, is superb. Scarlatti, Bellini, Verdi and Donizetti were all amongst its Musical Directors.

THE SEAFRONT

Around the little peninsula (or through the tunnel) from the palace is the area of **Santa Lucia**, made famous by the lyrical romantic song. Its most dramatic feature is the city's oldest castle, the strangely named **Castel dell'Ovo** (Castle of the Egg), built on a little islet, just offshore, over the remains of a Roman villa and 5th-century monastery. The first castle on the site dates to the 9th century, but it has been blown up and remodelled several times over the centuries. Its current form, from the outside, is the one given to it in 1503. It was used as a military installation until 1975, when its latest restoration turned it into a conference centre. At its foot, the **Borgo Marinaro** (fisherman's quarter) has become a trendy marina, and is filled with restaurants.

VIEW FROM BENEATH

Some 2500 years ago, the earliest inhabitants of Naples discovered that the soft tufa rock on which the city stands was easily carved into anything from wine cellars and warehouses to tunnels and catacombs. Today, this network forms almost an entirely new level to the city. Tours leave every weekend from the Caffè Gambrinus, Piazza Trieste e Trento.

Opposite: *At the end of Via Partenope, on the waterfront, is the huge Baroque Fontana dell'Immacolatella, built in 1601 and sculpted by Pietro Bernini.*

On shore, the neighbouring area is an elegant seafront promenade. It was built, along with the whole district behind it, in the 19th-century, as the wealthier families moved out of the crowded city centre to what is still one of Naples' most desirable residential areas. Known as the **Lungomare**, the waterfront is a pleasant place for a stroll, but there are also one or two sights worth a visit. Not far from the castle is the **Fontana dell'Immacolatella** (Immacolata Fountain), which was sculpted in 1601 by Michaelangelo Naccherino and Pietro Bernini. Continue from here past several of the city's finest hotels, still

sumptuous with Belle Epoque splendour, past the Piazza Vittoria to the sadly scruffy **Villa Comunale**, which has been a public park since 1697. It is home to the city aquarium, a number of fountains and some pleasing sculptures .

Behind it, the **Museo Villa Pignatelli** (Riviera di Chiaia) is a fascinating museum, based on the private collection of the 18th–19th century paintings, sculptures and ceramics of Prince Diego Aragona Pignatelle Cortes. The neo-classical villa was built in 1826 by Pietro Valente for the British Acton family, and later became the property of the Rothschilds. The stables house a collection of carriages.

At the far end, beyond another grand square, Piazza della Repubblica, **Mergellina** is the closest thing Naples has to a seaside resort, with a marina, rows of seafront

---

POWER OF THE EGG

According to legend, first written down in the 14th century, the Latin poet Virgil, who was considered by many to be a sorcerer, placed a carafe containing a magic egg in the foundations of the strangely-named Castel dell'Ovo (Castle of the Egg). The city will survive without any great harm as long as the egg remains intact.

Right: *A spectacular view of the Bay of Naples. It is no wonder why all the major powers throughout the centuries have sought to control it.*

cafés and restaurants , and a holiday atmosphere. On the hill above is a park which is supposed to contain the tomb of the Latin poet, Virgil. He is not there, but the Sicilian poet, Giacomo Leopardi, is.

POSILLIPO

Beyond Mergellina, the road sweeps round up the cliff to the northern arm of the Bay of Naples and the residential suburb of **Posillipo** whose Greek name Pausilypon (meaning 'respite from anxieties') gives a remarkable clue to its role in Neapolitan life. Always a haven of tranquillity, from the 17th–19th centuries, this was the hangout of the local super-rich, who left behind some spectacular villas. Amongst the finest are Cosimo Fanzago's unfinished **Palazzo Donn'Anna** (1642), built for Donna Anna Carafa, wife of the Viceroy Filippo Ramiro Guzman; the **Villa di Sir William Hamilton**, most famous as the place where Nelson met Emma Hamilton at a dinner party thrown by her husband while the fleet was in town, the neoclassical **Villa Doria D'Angri**, the **Egyptianate Ara Votiva per I Caduti per la Patria**, begun as a mausoleum in 1883 but adopted by the city as a war memorial, and the **Villa Quercia**.

Sadly, they have been overwhelmed in recent years by highrise development and most are virtually invisible behind high hedges and fences. However the views from the clifftop road are incomparable and those who are prepared to walk down the steep cliff (actually the crater wall of a long dead volcano) find themselves on a charming seafront, based on the little fishing village of **Marechiaro**. The best way to see the villas is from the sea, on the Naples-Procida ferry.

ON THE CLIFFTOP

On top of the cliff behind the town is another of the city's most desirable residential areas, **Vomero**, reached by three funicular railways. It is worth going up for the views alone, but the area also has a couple of the city's finest sights. The star-shaped **Castel Sant'Elmo** (Via Tito Angelini), which totally dominates views of the city, was built in 1537–1546 by Pedro Scriba for Viceroy Toledo to guard the outer defensive wall of the city. There is little to see inside, although it does house temporary exhibitions, but the views are superb.

Just in front of it, the **Certosa di San Martino** (Monastery of St Martin; Largo San Martino 5) has been a museum since 1866. This magnificent Carthusian monastery was originally founded by Charles of Anjou, Duke of Calabria in 1325, although the current buildings date mainly to the 16th century. The monks of San Martino lived in high style, and from the 15th–19th centuries collected around them a wonderful array of paintings, sculpture, ceramics, glass, jewellery, *presepi* and other Neapolitan crafts, most of which fetched up in the quarters of the Prior, the only member of the order technically allowed contact with the outside world. His rooms, the **Quarto del Priore** and the extravagantly Baroque church are two highlights in a fabulous museum.

> **LOCK UP THE TROUBLEMAKERS**
>
> Built to defend Naples from its enemies, the Castel Sant' Elmo has never fired a shot in anger against an invader, but it did prove useful as a prison, housing amongst many others, the Renaissance philosopher, Tommaso Campanella. During the Napoleon-inspired Republican Masaniello Revolt of 1799, the viceroy sheltered here from the mob. Once the rebellion was crushed, many of the ringleaders were imprisoned behind its solid walls, as were the defeated members of the 19th-century Risorgimento.

Below: *The suburb of Posillipo, once housing the stunning villas of the elite, but now overrun with apartment buildings.*

ROYAL CHINA

In the mid-18th century, with the secret of porcelain newly arrived from China, crowned heads across Europe were quick to found factories, from Limoges to Meissen. Bourbon King Charles III was no different and, in 1743, he set up a pavilion for the Royal Factory in the grounds of Capodimonte. It produced a distinctive 'soft paste' porcelain with elaborate frills and designs. The king loved it so much that he took his factory back to Spain with him in 1759, but the Pavilion was reopened in 1771.

Below: *The Museo Nazionale di Capodimonte, offers an incredible collection of paintings, porcelain and decorative arts from the various royal residents.*

Nearby, it is also worth visiting the attractive neo-classical **Villa Floridiana**, home to the **Museo Nazionale della Ceramica Duca di Martina** (Duke of Martina National Ceramic Museum; Villa Floridiana, Vomero), with an interesting collections of ceramics, majolica, glass, leather, Gothic ivory, and enamels.

Further along the ridge, towards the south of the city, is the **Palazzo Capodimonte**, the most magnificent of the royal palaces in Naples, commissioned by Charles III in 1738 partly as a hunting lodge, but mainly to house the superb Farnese art collection left to him by his mother. It was an extravagant scheme, the vast palace surrounded by a gracious park, which included, amongst other things, a pheasantry, zoo (with lions and elephants) and a huge greenhouse for exotic fruit. In all, the project took nearly 100 years to complete. The grounds also became home to the royal porcelain works, producing some of Europe's most famous ceramics – seen in their full glory in the 3000 tiles of Capodimonte porcelain which line the palace's **Salotta di porcellana** (Porcelain Room). As the **Museo Nazionale di Capodimonte** (Capodimonte National Museum and Park; Via Miano 1), the palace now houses a superb collection of furniture, porcelain

Left: *The San Gennaro Catacombs are the burial site of the patron saint Gennaro. They date from the 2nd century and are decorated with early Christian frescoes and mosaics.*

and fine art, with works by Rafael, Botticelli, Lippi, Vasari, El Greco, Caravaggio, Breughel, and Goya amongst others.

On the slopes below, just to the north of the Archaeological Museum are the old city cemeteries, with several interesting churches and intriguing, if sometimes rather grizzly, catacombs such as the huge two-storey **Catacombe di San Gennaro** (Via Capodimonte 13). Carved from the soft volcanic rock, this web of tunnels has been in use since the 2nd century, but acquired a desirable reputation when San Gennaro, patron saint of Naples, was buried here in the 6th century. All bishops of Naples were buried here until the 11th century amidst some fine 2nd–10th century frescoes and mosaics.

To the east, for a little light relief, is the **Orto Botanico** (Botanical Gardens, Via Foria 223), a lovely 12ha (30 acre) botanical garden, laid out by Joseph Bonaparte in 1807.

To the south, back at the gates of the old city, near the **Porta San Gennaro**, is the imposing **Church of San Giovanni a Carbonara** (Via San Giovanni a Carbonara 5), founded as an Augustin monastery in 1343. Highlights include its magnificent early 18th-century grand double staircase, designed by Ferdinando Sanfelice; paintings by Mattia Preti, added in 1656 as thanks for surviving the plague; the huge monumental tomb of King Ladislas (1414); the Tuscan tiled floor of the round Cappella Caracciolodel Sole (1427); and the paintings in the Cappella Caracciolo di Vico (1517).

TOURISM OF DEATH

There are several more interesting sites near the San Gennaro Catacombs. The San Severo Catacombs (Piazza San Severo) grew up around the tomb of San Severo, Bishop of Naples (AD364–410). The Basilica di Santa Maria della Sanità (Via Sanità 124) houses the relics of a popular local saint, San Vincenzo. Under the high altar, there is access to yet more catacombs, based around the burial site of an African bishop, Settimio Celio Gaudioso who died in exile in Naples in AD452. The Cimitero delle Fontanelle (Fontanelle Cemetery; Via Fontanelle 77) is a series of large caverns hewn from the rock for mass burials of victims of the 1836 cholera epidemic.

Naples at a Glance

BEST TIMES TO VISIT

The ideal time to visit Naples is in the **spring** (April-May) and **autumn** (September-October). However, if you don't want to swim, this really is a year-round destination. The **winters** are mild and can even be sunny, and the city hotels, restaurants and sights stay open all year. **Mid-summer** (July-August) can be very hot and overcrowded.

GETTING THERE

See Travel Tips, page 123.

GETTING AROUND

Naples centre is surprisingly small and you can do much of your sightseeing on foot. However, the city has an excellent public transport network combining buses, metros, funiculars (up to Vomero), trams (along the shoreline) and suburban trains. Ask the tourist office for a transport map. Use the same tickets, called Giranapoli, on everything. Buy them in advance from stations, tobacconists or newsagents and date stamp them the first time you use them to validate them. A single allows 90 minutes of travel; a full day ticket is good value if you are travelling a lot. If you are there for over 10 days, a monthly pass is cost-effective. Don't fare dodge – there are regular ticket inspections and stiff on-the-spot fines. Taxis are available on the street, but it is easier to call one. **Radio Taxi Partenope**, tel: 081-560 6666/556 0202.

WHERE TO STAY

The best place to stay is along the Lungomare, but also consider some of the pensions and small hotels in the old town and the Via Chaia area, and some grand old ladies on the Vomero slopes. There are cheaper hotels around the station, but walking around at night here can be dangerous.

LUXURY

Excelsior, Via Partenope 48, tel: 081-764 0111, fax: 081-764 9743. Belle Époque seafront hotel. Spacious and elegant rooms, flawless service. Guests include royalty, artists, film stars and politicians. The hotel restaurant, the **Casanova Grill**, is one of Naples' finest.
Grand Hotel Vesuvio, Via Partenope 45, tel: 081-764 0044, fax: 081-764 4483. It opened on the waterfront in 1882 and still retains its elegance. The great tenor, Enrico Caruso, died here in 1921.

MID-RANGE

Paradiso, Via Catullo 11, Posillipo, tel: 081-247 5111, fax: 081-761 3449. 74 good rooms, excellent food, and a stunning location. Sit on the terrace with the whole bay at your feet.
Pinto Storey, Via Martucci 72, tel: 081-681 260, fax: 081-667 536. Delightful little hotel on the 3rd floor of a mansion block on Piazza Amedeo. Charm, antiques and a good location.

BUDGET

Ausonia, Via Caracciolo 11, Mergellina, tel: 081-682 278, fax: 081-664 536. Small and popular, in an old mansion block, its marine décor reflects the nearby Mergellina seafront.
Hotel Duomo, Via Duomo 228, tel: 081-265 988. Small, family-run, in 19th-century building in the old town. Basic but pleasant and friendly.
Pensione Margherita, via Cimarosa 29, tel: 081-556 7044. Charming little pension near the Vomero funicular. Friendly, with spacious rooms and great views across the bay.
Soggiorno Sansevero, Via San Domenico Maggiore 9, tel: 081-551 5949. Pension in an 18th-century building in the old town. 6 rooms – so book early.

WHERE TO EAT

LUXURY

Da Dora, Via F. Palasciano 28, tel: 081-680 519. Delectable seafood in a charming family-run trattoria. Closed Sunday; and for 15 days in August.
Ciro a Santa Brigida, Via Santa Brigida 71, tel: 081-552 4072. A fantastic restaurant first opened in the 1930s. Two other branches, in Mergellina and the Borgo Marinaro.
La Sacrestia, Via Orazio 116, Posillipo, tel: 081-664 186. Lusciously inventive food, elegant décor and a garden terrace overlooking the bay. Very fashionable, so book ahead. Closed Monday and, Sunday in summer.

Naples at a Glance

MID-RANGE

La Cantina di Triunfo, Riviera di Chiaia 64, tel: 081-668 101. Mouthwatering variations on Neapolitan *cicuna povera*, plus delicious desserts, a superb wine list and home-made grappa.

Osteria dell'Arte, Via Rampe SG Maggiore 1/A, tel: 081-552 7558. Friendly inn. Watch out for the tripe and pigs' trotters lurking on the menu. Small and popular, so book ahead.

BUDGET

Osteria Mattonella, Via G. Nicotera 13, tel: 081-416 541. Nice, friendly family-run restaurant, with wooden tables, blue tiled walls and an ever changing selection of traditional food. Book ahead.

Pizzeria Brandi, Salita S, Anna di Palazzo 1/2 (cnr via Chiaia), tel: 081-416 928. In 1889, the *Margherita* pizza was invented here to celebrate the visit of Queen Margherita.

Pizzeria da Michele, Via Cesare Sersale 1–3, tel: 081-553 9204. Locals say these are the best pizzas in Naples, but only in two flavours – marinara or margherita. Cheap, noisy and cheerful. Closed Sunday.

Cafés

Gran Caffé Gambrinus, Piazza Trieste e Trento, tel: 081-417 582. Magnificently sumptuous coffee shop, a Neapolitan institution since 1866, and still the haunt of high society ladies who lunch.

Pasticceria Scaturchio, Piazza San Domenico Maggiore 19, tel: 081-551 6944. Old town patisserie. Sit in the square, watch the Sunday market and nibble a **ministeriali** (cake).

CLUBS AND BARS

Dizzy Club, Corso Vittorio Emanuele 19–20. Chess, cards and cocktails. Open 20:00–02:00. Closed Wednesday.

Caffè Megaride, Via Eldorado 1, Borgo Marinara, tel: 081-764 5300. The ideal place in the small hours, listening to the murmur of a gentle sea breeze.

Otto Jazz Club, Salita Cariati 23, Corso V. Emanuele, tel: 081-552 4373. Jazz and blues.

SHOPPING

You can buy almost anything here and often for very reasonable prices – look for Italian designer clothes in the Via Chaia area. For secondhand and antiquarian books, try Via Port d'Alba, next to Piazza Dante. For food, try the delicatessens along Spaccanapoli or the back street markets in the old town. For almost anything, the main shopping street in the city is Via Toledo.

TOURS AND EXCURSIONS

Consortaxi, Piazza S. Maria La Nova 44, tel: 081-552 0205; Numero Verde: 1670-16221. Tours by taxi of Naples and the surrounding region, including Sorrento, the Amalfi Coast, Pompeii and Herculaneum.

Chamber of Commerce Tours. Free city and area tours every Friday night and two Saturdays a month. Tickets from travel agents or hotels; commentary in Italian, English, French, and German.

USEFUL CONTACTS

Tourist Information:
Piazza del Gesù, tel: 081-523 328.
Website: www.regione.camponia.it
Toll-free helpline:
Hello Napoli, Numero Verde, 167-251 396. In Italian, English, French and German.
Provincial Tourist Office:
Piazza dei Martiri 58, Cap 80121, tel: 081-405 311, fax: 081-401 961. Kiosks also at:
Stazione Mergellina, tel: 081-761 2102; **Aeroporto Capodichino**, tel: 081-785 761; and **Stazione Centrale** FS, tel: 081-268 779.

NAPLES	J	F	M	A	M	J	J	A	S	O	N	D
AVERAGE TEMP. °C	8	9	11	14	17	21	24	24	21	17	13	10
AVERAGE TEMP. °F	46	48	52	57	63	70	75	75	70	63	56	50
HOURS OF SUN DAILY	4	4	5	7	8	9	10	10	8	6	4	3
RAINFALL mm	116	85	73	62	44	31	19	32	64	107	147	135
RAINFALL ins.	4.6	3.4	2.9	2.4	1.7	1.2	0.8	1.3	2.5	4.2	5.8	5.3
DAYS OF RAINFALL	11	10	9	8	7	4	2	3	5	9	11	12

3
North and West Naples

The peninsula that reaches out into the sea and forms the beautiful northern arm of the Bay of Naples, has been popular amongst the wealthy and fishermen since the Greeks arrived in the 8th century BC. Most of its towns have now been subsumed into ribbon development, but there are still many wonderful, often sadly disregarded sights.

THE CAMPI FLEGREI

Beyond **Posillipo**, the peninsula is known as the **Campi Flegrei** (Phlegraean or 'burning' Fields). Effectively, it sits on a giant pool of molten magma, which feeds at least 50 small volcanoes. The ancient world considered it to be a mystical location. **Lago d'Averna**, near **Pozzuoli**, is really a flooded crater, with particularly dark, lonely and atmospheric waters. Birds flying over were often asphyxiated by fumes, and thus it was regarded by both Homer and Virgil as the actual mouth of Hades (a concept that continued well into the middle ages, when Dante used it as the inspiration for his Inferno). Astonishingly, neither this nor the very real risk of eruption stopped people from settling here. At first, the Romans and Greeks set up spas, baths and temples near the hot springs, while the fertile volcanic soil encouraged the farmers and agricultural development. In recent years, it has become one of the city's most sought after commuter districts. Even more astonishingly, considering the high risks, the area is home to much of Naples's heavy industry, from steel and cement works, to chemical plants.

DON'T MISS

*** Caserta: home to one of Europe's largest and most ostentatious, if not most beautiful palaces.
*** Montecassino: a grand Benedictine monastery, lavishly endowed with beautiful art.
** Pozzuoli: the bubbling steaming Solfatara.
** Avellino, Aversa and other small towns: dot the routes north of Naples, and you should not miss a visit to antique **Capua** with its unusual town plan.

Opposite: *Fine Roman architecture is displayed in the Anfiteatro Flavio.*

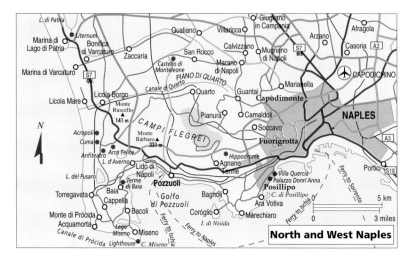

North and West Naples

POZZUOLI

Although probably first inhabited in the 7th century BC, it was in 530BC that some Samian exiles founded the first official town of **Dikaiarchia**. The town flourished, becoming an important trade and industrial centre under the Romans, who arrived in 194BC and changed its name to **Puteoli**. Amongst its more lucrative contracts was landing all the wheat consumed by Rome, imported from the Eastern Empire. By the 5th century AD, the barbarians arrived and its fortunes declined. The level of the land dropped by 12m (39ft) between the 2nd century BC and the 11th century AD, and the harbour silted up, then drowned. The land only began to rise again in the 17th century.

Today, the reason most people visit Pozzuoli is to see the extraordinary **Solfatara** (Via Solfatara 161), a shallow volcanic crater about 2km (1.5 miles) in diameter. Although it was formed about 4000 years ago and last erupted in AD1198, it still provides the most visible volcanic activity in the region. It has an entertaining collection of fumaroles (jets of steam and carbon dioxide), solfataras (jets of water vapour and sulphuric acid), bubbling sand, burping pools of boiling mud and colourful sulphur-yellow or reddish-purple stained rocks.

TIDAL TOWN

The **height** of the land around the **Campi Flegrei** has **fluctuated** over the centuries by several metres, according to the level of the giant magma pool on which the area rests. Since the 1960s, the level of this **seismic activity** (known as bradyseism) has been increasing steadily and the pool is now so full that the town of **Pozzuoli** has physically **risen** by nearly 8m (26ft).

Relatively few of the ancient city's civic buildings
have survived. The exception is the remarkably preserved **amphitheatre** (Via Terracciano), built in AD69–79.
Seating 40,000 people, it had a sophisticated system of
underground storage and mechanical trapdoors and
elevators, used when staging wild animal spectaculars.
Near the harbour, another fine Roman building was long
thought to be the Temple of Serapide, but is now known
to have been the rather more prosaic **Macellum** or city
market (Piazza Serapide).

Unfortunately, due to the seismic upheavals, the
pretty **Rione Terra** (old town) near the harbour had to
be evacuated in 1970. Restoration work is now under-
way, but until the district and its buildings have been
properly stabilized, they remain off limits.

> **Top Tip**
>
> Although the **Cumana train**
> stops in **Pozzuoli**, it is better
> to take a **bus** from the **Lun-
> gomare** in Naples to the
> entrance of the **Solfatara**,
> then go on to visit the town.
> This means that you can
> do the steep walk downhill
> and take the train back into
> Naples from the town centre.

CUMA

As the road heads west across the neck of the peninsula,
along the old Roman Via Domitiana, it passes a grand
triumphal arch, the **Arco Felice**, and Lago d'Averno.
Cuma is believed to be one of the oldest settlements in
southern Italy. Until about the 3rd century BC, it reigned
supreme but declined rapidly as Puteoli (Pozzuoli)
flourished. Relatively small areas have yet to be fully

Below: *Visit Solfatara,
a large volcanic crater. It
now lies dormant, but it
is still possible to see forms
of volcanic activity in the
jets of steam, sulphur
vapours and boiling mud.*

Below: *The 1st-century Flavian amphitheatre in Pozzuoli was very impressive, seating up to 40,000 spectators.*

excavated, but the **Parco Archeologico** (Via Acropoli) is still impressive, with temples to Jupiter and Apollo. The only thing to keep the town on the Roman map was the presence of an Oracle. The **Antro della Sibilla** (Sibyl's Grotto) is a cave carved from the soft tufa, which was supposedly home to virgin priestesses of the Cult of Apollo. According to the Aeneid, Aeneas was one of the many people who travelled long distances to visit them. Other, more likely explanations for the excavations range from a Greek tomb to military defensive tunnels.

BAIA

Turn south instead onto the peninsula and there are several interesting small towns. The Roman fleet was based at **Miseno**, but the area has been continuously inhabited since and relatively little remains of their installations. Their greatest legacy is their massive underground water storage cistern, the **Piscina Mirabile** (Via A. Greco), carved from the tufa at **Bacoli**. Measuring 70m x 25.5m x15m, with a vaulted ceiling resting on 48 giant pillars, it is the largest known Roman reservoir in the world.

Baia was a popular Roman spa, the favoured watering hole of emperors Caligula, Claudius, Nero and

Domitian. Much of it is sadly now underwater, but there are still many imposing remains, of which the finest are probably the **Terme Romana** (Roman Baths, Via Fusaro 35). The **Museo Archeologico dei Campi Flegrei** (Phlegraean Fields Archaeology Museum), home to most of the archaeological finds from the area, is housed in a

spectacular fortress. The fortress, **Castello Aragonese** was built in 1538 by the Spanish viceroy, don Pedro de Toledo, around a medieval core.

Above: *The Flavian amphitheatre contained a network of underground cells. Wild animals were kept in these cells, and used to fight as part of the entertainment.*

CAPUA

Best known from Shakespeare, stories of ancient glory abound in Capua – it was here that Hannibal dallied in a luxurious life, while its gateway marked the edge of the Holy Roman Empire (sculptures are preserved in the Museum). The Roman town lies just beyond the borders of the 'modern' Capua, constructed in a tight net of narrow arched streets within an unusual triangular plan. Many of its buildings are made of Roman stone. The cathedral is a compilation of periods, much rebuilt since construction 11 centuries ago. Even then, bits were recycled – some of its Corinthian columns belong to 3rd century Rome, rather than the Romanesque. Around the cathedral, narrow alleys and churches are packed into the confines of the old ramparts. Don't miss the **Piazza Giudici** with a baroque church, and the town hall.

The **Museo Campano**, an excellent small museum at the corner of the Via Duomo, houses a collection of sculpture in its medieval section, and mosaics, too. There is something really unusual here however – a large and fascinating collection of sculptures of earth goddesses over 2000 years old. The oldest dates to the 7th century BC.

CAPUA

Capua may be redolent of Rome but it has much more history to offer. The site itself is an ancient one, and has been lived on for thousands of years, as revealed by a fascinating and varied collection of earth goddesses of the 7th to the 1st century BC. These can be seen at the Museo Campano, by the Via Duomo. There are also fine sculptures from the date of 1239, marking the boundary of an emperor's lands.

Above: *The Caserta Royal Palace is more impressive because of its actual size than its beauty. However, the opulent 18th-century Royal Apartments, the Court Theatre and the lovely gardens are definitely worth visiting.*

Opposite: *The elaborate interior of the Royal Palace cannot fail to impress.*

CASERTA

In 1750, Bourbon King Charles III, looked enviously on Versailles and began to spend. Choosing a site safely inland, he commissioned locally born painter, Luigi Vanvitelli, to create for him the palace to put all others in the shade. Construction went ahead at full speed for over 20 years, before limping on into the following century. What Vanvitelli created is extraordinary more for its size than its beauty. The Royal Palace (measuring a staggering 247m x 184m) has 34 staircases linking 1200 rooms, arranged around four identical courtyards. It is nearly double the size of Versailles, although only half that of the Bourbons' other monstrosity, the Escorial, near Madrid. Unusually, the public façade is far less decorative than the back elevation, designed to be seen only by the court. Only the royal apartments and the gardens are open to the public, but still allow a full day's touring.

The many carvings, sculptures, paintings, panels, gilded furnishing and elaborate marble halls are all designed to impress and they cannot fail to do so – although sadly, more for their opulence than their artistic merit. The highlights undoubtedly are the magnificent grounds, with formal vistas and walkways, fountains and lakes, and a luxuriantly planted English garden. For those with weary feet, there is a bus which runs around the grounds to various key points.

During World War II, the palace was used as the **Allied Military Headquarters** and it was here that Germany officially surrendered in 1945.

The town that grew up around the palace is uninspiring, but 10km (6 miles) away, on the slopes of Mount Virgo is **Caserta Vecchia**. This charming, sleepy old place was probably founded by the Lombards in the 8th century. Because it has virtually been ignored since the 18th century, its medieval centre, clustered around a beautiful 12th-century cathedral, has survived almost intact.

NORTH TO SESSA AURUNCA

In the extreme west of Campania, below the hills and above Capua and Caserta, this stretch of coast running as far as the border with Lazio, is often overlooked. You can drive along a shore road, the S7, or ascend inland through fine scenery as far as **Sessa Aurunca**, which is

GLORIOUS GARDENS

Caserta's gardens remind you of another time – a melancholic lost world which was a backdrop for 18th-century Neapolitan fops and their ladies. This ghostly French garden with its monumental sculpture rising along parterres and above pools, specimen trees, fountains that once played to the Bourbon court, sombre allées and vistas, is perhaps the most touching image that people take away from this rather heavy and ponderous palace of pleasure.

MONTECASSINO

It is hard to believe the building was ruined by bombardments in World War II. It has actually been destroyed four times since being established as the mother house of the Benedictine order in AD 529. The hard-fought offensive of 1943–4 lasted eight months after the Allies had liberated Naples. It is much visited by old soldiers, American, British, Polish and French; the last two armies suffered particularly. The Nazi forces quitted the abbey on 17 May 1945, leaving open the road to Rome

Below: *A splendid fountain in the Caserta gardens.*

a town of Roman origins with important remains of the period – notably a theatre and a bath-house as well as a fine Roman bridge outside the little town. It is a particularly colourful place with its green and yellow roof tiles and its 12th-century cathedral decorated with fine bas reliefs. There is a ruined castle too, beyond the centre, sternly medieval with a square tower. A quiet and large beach called **Baia Domizia**, can be reached just below Sessa.

After a visit to Sessa Aurunca go on down 6km (4 miles) to the small town of **Carinola**. The medieval town also has a castle whose notable 15th-century duomo owes much of its design to the vast hilltop abbey of Montecassino, in nearby Lazio. The motherhouse of the Benedictine order, containing the tomb of St Benedict, Montecassino dominates the surrounding area. An amazing aspect is the steep road climbing the hill. Once at the abbey be prepared for the most sumptuous interiors with much use of marble, stucco and gilding in the reconstructed church. In the **museum** are works of art that escaped the heavy bombardment to which the abbey was subject in 1944 before being captured by the Allies.

Other interesting towns up from the coast are **Teano**, with a Roman ampitheatre which dates from just after Hannibal sacked the town around the 4th century BC. **Calvi** has a near-complete Roman town laid out beside its cathedral. If you want to get to **Roccamonfina** at the base of Monte Ste Croce, walk through deep chestnut woods to see a notable cloister at the Monastery Santa Maria.

North and West of Naples at a Glance

Spring and autumn are ideal, with warm weather and plenty of sunshine. Mid-summer can be too hot and crowded for heavy-duty sight-seeing. The area remains mild in winter and this really is a year-round destination.

GETTING THERE

There are two privately operated railway lines, the Circumflegrea, from and Ferrovia Cumana along the northern arm of the Bay, linking Naples with the various towns to the west, including Pozzuoli and Cumae. Both depart from Montesanto Station (tel: 081-551 3328) every 10–20mins. For Solfatara, however, it is best to take the bus from the Lungomare in Naples to the entrance of the Solfatara, when finished there continue down to Pozzuoli railway station. It will save you a long, steep walk up hill. Giranapoli tickets accepted on bus and trains. The easiest way to get to Caserta, 27km (17 miles) from Naples, is by train from the Central Station. From Caserta, there are regular buses to Capua, but you will need a car or taxi to visit Caserta Vecchia.

WHERE TO STAY

LUXURY
The Grand Hotel Vanvitelli, Viale Carlo III, 81020 S, San Marco Evangelista (Ce), tel: 0823-217 111, fax: 0823-421 330, or e-mail:

info@grandhotelvanvitelli.it Top class business-style hotel with luxurious rooms, near the Reggia. Swimmimg pool, garage and parking-lot.
Jolly Hotel Caserta, Via V Veneto 9, Caserta 81100, tel: 0823-325 222, fax: 0823-354 522. A comfortable, well-equipped chain hotel with full facilities, close to the Reggia.

MID-RANGE
Villa de Pertis Hotel, Via Ponti 30, S. Giorgio 81010, Dragoni, tel/fax: 0823-866 619. Restored country house hotel about 25km (16 miles) from Caserta, with panoramic views of the Matese Mountains. Terraced restaurant, good food.

BUDGET
Volcana Solfatara, Via Solfatara 16, Pozzuoli, tel: 081-526 7413. The nearest campsite to the centre of Naples.

WHERE TO EAT

LUXURY
La Rocca di S. Andrea dei Longobardi, Via Torre 8, Caserta Vecchia 81020, tel/fax: 0823-371 232. Lavish restaurant-pizzeria, with traditional local food, set in gardens with great views, 9km (6 miles) from Caserta. Closed Monday.
Ristorante La Paratella, Palazzina Borbonica, Via Giardini Reali 1, San Leucio di Caserta, tel: 0823-301 497, fax: 0823-362 277, or e-mail: info@paratella.it Charming, on a hilltop in a

restored 18th-century palazzo. Terrace, gardens and fine local cuisine. Closed Tuesday.

MID-RANGE
Antica Locanda, Piazza della Seta, Caserta, tel: 0823-305 444. Recommended trattoria in Caserta, serving a mix of pasta and seafood. Excellent. Closed Sunday lunch and Monday, and from 8-22 August.
Azienda Agrituristica Il, Asolare, Via Selvatico, Contrada Coste dei Fondi di Báia, Báia 80070, tel: 081-523 5193. A delightful small restaurant with four charmingly decorated bedrooms inside a now extinct volcanic crater near Baia, between Pozzuoli and Cumae. The food is traditional Neapolitan. No credit cards. Book ahead. No dinner on Sunday. Closed Monday.
Antica Trattoria Da Ciuffello, Via Dicearchia 11 bis, Pozzuoli, tel: 081-526 9397. Attractive little trattoria near the macellum, which specializes in seafood, with a fish barbecue and a delicious fish soup. Closed Wednesday and in winter.

USEFUL CONTACTS

Tourist Information
Caserta
Piazza Dante 35, tel: 0823-321 1371.
Pozzuoli
Via Campi Flegrei 3, tel: 081-526 2419, fax: 081-526 1481. Piazza Matteotti 1/a, tel: 081-526 6639.

4
Under the Volcano

South of the city, the **Bay of Naples** stretches out in a long curve, its flat coastal farmlands totally dominated by the giant, rust-red cone of Mount Vesuvius, the last active volcano on mainland Europe and probably the most famous in the world. It has rumbled and grumbled a lot over the millennia but its infamy really stems from one particularly vicious eruption in AD79 when it buried the thriving Roman towns of Pompeii and Herculaneum, preserving them for posterity in ash and mud. Today, Pompeii is, without doubt, the most complete and exciting ancient city in the world, and while much of Herculaneum remains buried under modern Ercolano, now a suburb of expanding Naples, the relatively small area of excavations open to the public is a compelling glimpse of everyday life, Roman-style. Allow at least two days to explore the area.

VESUVIO (VESUVIUS)
Although the whole Bay of Naples rests on a sea of molten lava, from the Campi Flegrei to the north west of Naples to the thermal springs of Ischia, Mount Vesuvius is the undoubted king, a towering cone that has spewed romance and tragedy into the local air again and again through the centuries. The volcano's spirit is a lively one and locals are never sure when the mountain will perform again. The last seismic activity in the area was a relatively mild earthquake in 1980, but there hasn't been an eruption since 1944. There was severe damage to property, but the slow-moving lava field allowed all but 27 people, killed by falling masonry, to reach safety.

DON'T MISS

*** **Pompeii**: Rome's finest legacy, trapped in time under volcanic mud and ash.
*** **Mt Vesuvius**: The volcano responsible for destroying Pompeii and Herculaneum, mainland Europe's last active volcano.
*** **Ercolano**: (Herculaneum) A Roman resort town, now a suburb of Naples, also frozen by the eruption of AD79.

Opposite: *A statue found at Ercolano (Herculaneum). The town was destroyed in 79AD, during the eruption of Vesuvius.*

Above: *The ancient site of Herculaneum is situated below the modern town. Even though the area is still being excavated, it gives a good impression of the town plan.*

Mount Vesuvius (1281m/4203ft) first blew itself into existence about 12,000 years ago. Since then it has erupted regularly, with over 100 recorded eruptions since AD79, although only those in 1631, 1794 and 1944 have caused severe damage. Today, only a wisp of smoke deep inside the high crater shows a glimmer of life, but vulcanologists are far from sanguine. About 8km (5 miles) below the surface, the magma chamber is as active as ever, with molten lava climbing slowly up the pipe. There is little sign of it because the last eruption plugged the top of the pipe and geologists fear that next time the mountain blows, it will do so with the explosive force of a giant pressure cooker, literally lifting the top off the mountain.

It was this type of explosion which caused such devastation on the 24th August, AD79, when a mushroom cloud shot over 30km (19 miles) into the air, and several metres of asphyxiating ash and pumice rained down on Pompeii. A couple of days later, as the wind died, the cloud collapsed and a tidal wave of superheated rock, ash and dust, reaching temperatures of over 475°C (887°F), swept down the slopes at 160kph (100mph). It was this pyroclastic flow that finally buried the stunned cities, killing thousands as it passed. The horror was unimaginable then – but this time there are potentially nearly 3 million people living in the path of destruction, and the only evacuation plan is ill-conceived and unworkable, based on two weeks' notice of an eruption. Anything better will take some 10 years to put into place.

A TOUGH HIKE

There used to be a chair lift to the top of Mount Vesuvius, but since it collapsed, ecologists seem bizarrely to feel that the tramp of hundreds of weary feet is better for the environment. Now the only way to get to the top (1281m/ 4163ft) is on foot. The path is only about 600m (650 yd) long, but it winds steeply up the slope and takes most people 30–45 minutes. Avoid the midday heat as there is no shade. Wear sensible walking shoes, a hat and take some water.

Yet nothing seems to deter locals and visitors alike. More and more houses are built on the slopes, while hundreds flock up the mountain each day to see the magnificent views and stare awe-struck into the depths of the huge crater, 200m (656ft) deep and 600m (1969ft) in diameter. Those with the time can walk right around the rim, but it is no longer possible to climb down inside.

On the way down, try and stop at the **Osservatorio Vesuviana** (Vesuvius Observatory), where there is a fascinatingly multi-coloured collection of volcanic rocks on display. It was built as a research centre by Ferdinand II in 1841–1845 and is still in use today.

ERCOLANO (HERCULANEUM)

From Ercolano station, walk down the hill about 300m (329yd) to the gate of Herculaneum, said by ancient historian Dionysius of Halicarnassos to have been founded by Heracles (Hercules) himself. The view from above gives a remarkable insight into the town plan, even though a relatively small area has been excavated – modern Ercolano is built on top of much of the ancient city. Herculaneum is far smaller than Pompeii, but in many ways it is just as atmospheric and more friendly on the feet – you can explore it easily within a couple of hours.

> **EXPLOSIVE OFFSPRING**
>
> Huge, cone-shaped Mount Vesuvius actually stands inside the crater of a much larger, much earlier volcano, Monte Somma, a giant which was thought to have been formed about 12,000 years ago and been three times the height at nearly 2000m (6562ft). Look to your left as you drive up the hill and you can see part of the rounded crater walls of the ancient mountain, which collapsed during the AD79 eruption. The area is now run as a nature reserve.

The town's early history is unclear, but it was probably founded in the 7th century BC. Until AD 79, Herculaneum and Pompeii both stood on the seashore – the eruption dropped so much mud and rock into the water that it pushed the shore back by nearly 2km

(1.2 miles). The Romans arrived in about 290BC, and the town became a thriving holiday resort, with a population of about 5000. It was of less importance than Pompeii, but popular amongst patrician families who knocked down the seaward wall to give their villas uninterrupted views.

Herculaneum was never buried under the initial carpet of ash that fell on Pompeii. For years archaeologists believed that the people had managed to escape the catastrophe of the eruption as only six bodies were found in the streets. In the 1980s, new excavations uncovered the ghastly truth. As the boiling mud cascaded through the streets, the residents fled towards the water where they were trapped, taking refuge in the seafront warehouses below the patrician villas, now grimly full of hundreds of badly burned skeletons.

The lava flow proved far more kind to posterity and many of the houses and shops here have survived remarkably intact, with second-storeys, wooden balconies, doors, staircases and wall paintings still

Right: *The Casa del Bel Cortile (House of the Beautiful Courtyard) in Herculaneum was excavated in the 18th-century.*

in situ. In one house, 18th-century archaeologists discovered a library of 2000 papyrus scrolls. If you lift up your eyes, the ancient streets merge remarkably with those of the modern town. Surprisingly little has changed here in the last 2000 years.

Take time to wander the streets, peering into houses so vividly alive it seems as if the residents have just popped out for a minute. Some are highly decora-tive, such as the wealthy **Casa dell'Albergo**, the **Casa di Nettuno e Anfitrite** (House of the Neptune and Amphitrite Mosaic), whose summer dining room is lav-ishly ornamented by mosaic, the obviously-named **Casa del Atrio o Mosaico** (House of the Mosaic Atrium), and the **Casa del Rilievo di Telefo** (House of the Relief of Telephus), with magnificent marble decoration, includ-ing a bas-relief of the myth of Telephus. Many of the frescoes show signs of restoration, following an earth-quake in AD63 which caused a great deal of structural damage. Many fine sculptures, including two elegant statues of stags found in the **Casa dei Cervi** (House of the Stags) are now in the Naples museum.

The forum and main public buildings have never been found, although archaeologists have a good idea of where they are. The public face of the city is most evident in the two **Terme** (Baths), remarkably similar to a modern Turkish Bath, with separate sections for men and women, hot, tepid and cold pools and a central courtyard for social lounging. Several apartment blocks and shops, such as the **Casa a Graticcio** and three-storey **Casa del Tramezzo di Legno**, are instantly recognizable while the large **palaestra** (gymnasium), to the far side of the site, has a temple, pools, training grounds and offices. The theatre is visitable, just to the left of the main site, off the road to Naples.

Above: *The Casa di Nettuno e Anfitrite (The House of Neptune and Amphitrite) takes its name from the blue and green mosaic of Neptune and Amphitrite found on the shrine wall at the back of the house.*

ROYAL FASCINATION

Charles, the Bourbon king of Naples, who was a great devotee of history, funded the first proper archaeo-logical studies of Pompeii in 1738. Fascinated by the volcano and the excavations, he chose to build his new palace at nearby Portici, creating at the same time the Palazzo Caramanico as an archaeological museum. In his footsteps trailed the nobility who built a series of magnificent, if now sadly crumbling, 18th- and 19th-century villas. These villas stretch along what is now known as the Miglio d'Oro (Golden Mile).

Above Right: *Stroll down the Via dei Sepolcri in ancient Pompeii.*
Opposite: *The amphitheatre at Pompeii was used for gladiatorial battles.*

SOUTH ALONG THE COAST

The coast road, the S18, south of Ercolano winds round the foot of the mountain through several interesting little towns. The first stretch passes the run-down 18th-century villas of the **Miglio d'Oro** (Golden Mile) on its way into Portici, whose 17th-century incarnation featured in Auber's opera Muette di Portici. In the 18th century, King Charles built a new palace, the Reggia, here, close to his beloved excavations. In 1839, Italy's first railway line was completed, linking the royal palaces in Naples and Portici.

The **Reggia** (Via Università 100, Portici) escaped the terminal decay of most of the surrounding villas by housing the local Department of Agriculture. It was recently restored to full glory and is open by appointment or for special exhibitions. The only other local villa that you can visit is the **Villa Campolieto** (Corso Resina 283, Ercolano) which also hosts a summer arts festival.

A little further south, **Torre de Greco**, named after the surrounding 'Greek' vineyards, also lay in the path of several eruptions – it has several times been laid to waste by the volcano but always rises again. Interestingly its many souvenir shops make use of volcanic stone as well as coral to make brooches and beads.

Torre Annunziata has also has also been in the direct line of the fire, often destroyed yet just as constantly revived. Here factories turn out streams of pasta. It is more notable (certainly more interesting) for being the location of an ancient Roman house, the **Villa Oplontis** (Via Sepolcri 1), which is open to the public and well worth a stop. A large, well excavated structure, it shows the sites of the slave quarters and also that of the Empress – it reputedly belonged to Poppaea, wife of Nero. The villa is noted for its carefully conserved wall paintings, landscapes, portraits, flowers and fountains with the peacock a frequent image.

POMPEII

First founded in the 8th century BC by Greek settlers, the town, now far inland and dry, stood on the marshy curve of an oxbow lake at the mouth of the Sarno River. From the 6th century BC, it seems likely that there were Etruscan settlers in the area and from the 5th century BC, it was invaded by the Samnites, later coming under Roman supervision. It remained faithful to Rome during the Social War of 89BC, but followed the wrong man in an internal squabble soon afterwards and was conquered by the dictator Sulla after that. He placed his nephew in charge, renamed Colonia Veneria Cornelia Pompeii, after its conqueror, Pompey, and his favourite goddess, Venus, to whom he built a magnificent temple on the forum. Over the next few years, 2000 favoured legionaries

STURDY SHOES REQUIRED

Pompeii may not have been a huge city, but when you have a whole town to explore, it takes time. Go early and allow a whole day, take a hat, water, comfortable shoes, a good map and guidebook (available at the site). Don't believe those who say you can't enter a building except on a guided tour – just follow the group in front. If you do choose to do a tour, most last about two hours and follow one of three set routes around selected highlights.

were granted lands and property in and around the town. Gradually Roman and Samnite cultures merged. There is still clear evidence of both.

By the 1st century AD, Pompeii was a thriving market town with a population of about 10,000 (of whom about 60 per cent were freemen, the rest slaves), serving the local agricultural community and trading far afield. Surrounded by a 3km (2 mile) defensive wall, with eight city gates, the city is laid out on a classic grid of narrow paved streets surrounding a central forum. It had an excellent social life, with numerous inns and hotels, an amphitheatre (for spectaculars), theatre, smaller odeon, two gymnasia and a large forum surrounded by temples and imposing administrative buildings. It was also politically active, with election 'posters' found grafittied onto the walls. In AD62, the area was rocked by a massive earthquake and buildings were still being restored or replaced when the volcano erupted in AD79.

Destruction and Rediscovery

At first, as the mountain blew its top, a rain of ash fell upon the town burying it several metres deep, but it was not this which caused the final devastation. As archaeologists dug through the layers, they found evidence that people had managed to crawl out of hiding holes and

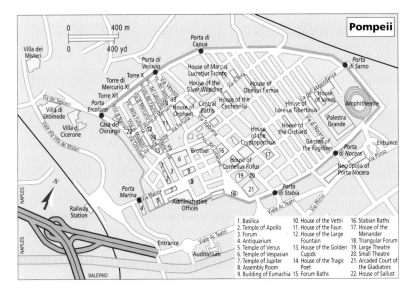

Pompeii

1. Basilica	10. House of the Vettii
2. Temple of Apollo	11. House of the Faun
3. Forum	12. House of the Large
4. Antiquarium	Fountain
5. Temple of Venus	13. House of the Golden
6. Temple of Vespasian	Cupids
7. Temple of Jupiter	14. House of the Tragic
8. Assembly Room	Poet
9. Building of Eumachia	15. Forum Baths

16. Stabian Baths
17. House of the
Menander
18. Triangular Forum
19. Large Theatre
20. Small Theatre
21. Arcaded Court of
the Gladiators
22. House of Sallust

up on top of the ash, bringing with them treasured possessions. In the calm before the ultimate storm, the citizens must have felt that however desperate the damage, they still had a chance to rebuild their lives. Then, as in Herculaneum, the pyroclastic flow struck the town, a flood of molten mud, rock and lava which hit without warning, searing the flesh from the terrified inhabitants as it swept across the town, and down to the sea. Some undoubtedly escaped, but evidence of more than 5000 bodies has been found to date.

The area remained inhabited, but the town was never rebuilt and over the centuries, it was completely forgotten. In the late 16th century, architect, Domenico Fontana, discovered a few inscriptions while building a tunnel, but nothing much more happened until 1748 when Bourbon King Charles III took personal charge. Since then, archaeologists have worked on the site, virtually without interruption. The whole town has been identified and around 80 per cent of it has been uncovered and restored. Most of the more fragile finds are now in the Archaeological Museum in Naples, but

---

THE LITTLE DETAILS

It is surprising to see what survived and what was preserved by the great eruption of Vesuvius in AD79. At Pompeii daily life is revealed, often touchingly, in stone streets rutted with cart tracks, gardens, fast food stalls, a beware of the dog sign, an unfinished plate of pasta and beans (still a local speciality), or the illicit presence of an elegant woman in the barracks of the gladiators that fatal afternoon.

Opposite: *In the Garden of Fugitives lie the plaster bodies of 27 people who fell while trying to flee the volcanic blast.*

there is still the most extraordinarily complete record of life – literally frozen on a single day. Even the thousands of tourists who flock here each year simply repeople the streets and add a realistic bustle to the proceedings.

Highlights

The main entrance to the site is through the ancient **Porta Marina** (Sea Gate) from where a main road leads straight up, past the **Basilica**, home of the law courts and administrative offices, and 3rd century BC **Temple of Apollo** to the **Forum**. This huge arcaded area (32m x 142m) was the central focus of the city, a combination of market, social hangout and official meeting place. Surrounding it are various important public buildings, including the **Antiquarium**. Rebuilt in 1948, it now houses a number of small finds, including the famous plaster casts of people and animals, the last few remnants of Sulla's famous **Temple of Venus**, along with **Temples to Vespasian and Jupiter**, three administrative offices, the **Assembly Room**, the **Building of Eumachia**, the home of the corporation of fullers and dyers used for public auctions, and the covered market.

Before heading further into town, turn left along the line of the walls and head out of the Porto Ercolano, down the statue-lined **Via dei Sepolcri**, through

Below: *The Forum served as the commercial, religious, and political centre of this Roman resort.*

the city's most affluent and beautiful cemetery to the magnificently decorated **Villa dei Misteri** (House of Mysteries). Originally built around the 2nd century BC, this was heavily restored in approximately 60BC and again just before the eruption. With the main rooms beautifully lined with figurative and *trompe l'oeil* fres-

coes, and a series of small courtyards and terraces that point to gracious living, this was also very much a working farm with wine presses and servants' quarters.

Thread your way back towards the forum through the narrow streets of Pompeii's wealthiest quarter, where the Vicolo di Mercurio, Via delle Terme and Via della Fortuna are home to several fine patrician villas. Those particularly worth a visit include the **House of the Vettii**, (currently under restoration), whose most famous decorations include a rather startling depiction of the well-endowed Priapus; the palatial **House of the Faun**, the largest house in Pompeii, covering nearly 3000m² (9843ft²), and home to one of the world's finest known mosaics, a huge tableau of Alexander the Great defeating the Persians at the battle of Issos; the **House of the Large Fountain**, the **House of the Golden Cupids**, and the **House of the Tragic Poet**, most famous for its mosaic 'Beware of the Dog' sign, now in the Naples museum. Just before you reach the Forum, on Via del Foro, you pass the modern restaurant/coffee shop and the ancient **Forum Baths**, a large, elaborate complex built soon after the Roman conquest, with fine stucco ornamentation, frescoes and mosaic floors.

From the forum, turn into **Via dell'Abbondanza** – Main Street, Pompeii. Quite extraordinarily complete, with many of its buildings still reaching double-storeys, this leads right across the city past a whole series of highly decorated villas, interspersed with shops. A short way down on the left hand-side, the Vicolo del Lupanare

FAST FOOD STALLS

On many of the street corners you will see counter tops with holes in them. These belonged to the city's thermopilia, or fast food stalls. Tiny, one-room outlets, open to the street, some had a few chairs, but most only had a counter with holes set in it for jars of food and drink, an oven behind to heat the food and water for hot wine in winter. Then, as now, the local café/bar was an integral part of Italian life.

Right: *The Terme Stabiane, or Stabian Baths are the oldest in the city of Pompeii, dating back to the 4th century* BC

leads to the graphically decorated **Brothel**. Back on the main road, a short distance further on, you come to the **Stabian Baths**, one of the oldest buildings in the city, originally built in the 3rd–4th century BC, but later expanded, renovated and redecorated, with a series of elaborate bathrooms surrounding a huge open courtyard or palaestra, used for physical exercise.

At the far end of Via dell'Abbondanza lies the huge oval **Amphitheatre**, the oldest known in the world, dating to 80–70BC, with space for about 20,000 spectators. Next to it, the **Palaestra Grande** (Large Palaestra or sports field) with a pool and exercise fields was built for military training and youthful gymnastics during the reign of Augustus. From here, Via di Nocera leads down to a city gate, while off to the right, circling the current excavations, you head for the **Garden of the Fugitives**, a former vineyard in which 27 contorted plaster bodies lie where the fleeing people fell.

Head back towards the main road, and walk back to the centre along the road parallel to Via dell'Abbondanza, passing two more particularly fine villas, the **House of the Menander**, and the **House of the Ceii**, with electioneering slogans still visible on the wall. Beyond these, Via Stabia leads down to the **Triangular Forum**, a small piazza at the centre of the entertainment quarter, surrounded by the **Theatre** (still used in summer), **Odeon** (originally used for concerts), and **Arcaded Court of the Gladiators**.

FIVE-STAR HOTEL

Classical remains are still being uncovered, and parts of Pompeii remain unexplored. The most recent discovery, announced in early 2000, was of an inn outside Pompeii. But what an inn! Buried under 4m (13ft) of solidified ash in the great eruption, and later flooded, this was described as being an hotel of great luxury, an establishment for wealthy visitors to the city. It contains five large reception rooms complete with dining couches, fountains, wide windows and wall paintings.

Under the Volcano at a Glance

The ideal time to visit here is in **spring** or **autumn**, before the searing heat and the crowds of **summer** appear, but it is still possible to visit at any time of year. If you are planning to climb Mount Vesuvius, it is best to do it early in the morning or late in the afternoon, when the light is better and the temperature kinder. Allow at least a full day to explore the area; preferably one day for Vesuvius and Herculaneum, a second full day for Pompeii.

The privately operated Circumvesuviana **train** (tel: 081-772 2444) runs around the bay, from Naples to Sorrento, with stops both at Ercolano, for Herculaneum and Vesuvius and Pompeii-Scavi-Villa dei Misteri station for Pompeii. Beyond Pompeii, the line branches and you may have to change trains at Torre Annunziata or wait for the correct service to get back to Sorrento. You can get a city **bus** (Giranapoli tickets acceptable) if travelling from Naples to Ercolano. If **driving**, always park in paid areas.

Vesuvius

Infrequent tourist buses head up the mountain from the entrance to the Herculaneum excavations (for information, tel: 081-882 6787, or ask the tourist office). However it is much easier, and not much more expensive to use one of the shared taxis in the station forecourt. They will wait for you up top. From the car park near the summit, there is a 600m (197ft) climb up to the crater rim. Wear stout comfortable shoes, and take a hat and something to drink.

Ercolano

The town buses stop beside the gates of the excavation; if coming from the station, walk downhill for about 300m (98ft). Open daily 09:00 until two hours before dusk, tel: 081-739 0963.

Pompeii

The main entrance is about 200m (66ft) from Pompeii Scavi–Villa dei Misteri station. Pompeii Town station is a long walk from the site, and if you leave by the Porta di Nocera at the far end of the site, you face a 2km (1 mile) walk back to the station, with no buses or taxis in sight. Open daily 09:00 until one hour before dusk. For admission, tel: 081-861 0744. June–September, evening *son et lumière* performances (tel: 081-854 5111 for details).

It is better to stay in one of the many wonderful hotels in Naples, Sorrento, the islands or Amalfi, rather than in this area. But is you wish to stay here, try:

MID-RANGE

Villa Laura, Via della Salle 13, Pompeii 80045, tel: 081-863 1024/36, fax: 081-850 4893. Small, attractive, family-run hotel with a lovely garden and parking.

BUDGET

Motel Villa dei Misteri, Via Villa dei Misteri 11, Pompeii, tel: 081-861 3593, fax: 081-862 2983. Cheerful small hotel about 100m (110yd) from station and main entrance to the excavations.

La Locanda di Annagrazia, Via Colle S. Bartolomeo 71, Pompeii, tel: 081-863 2505. An attractively decorated country restaurant with friendly service, traditional Neapolitan food, and wine grown on the slopes of Mount Vesuvius.
Trattoria da Addu' Mimi, Via Roma 61, Pompeii, tel: 081-863 8332. There is good pasta in this cheerful, basic trattoria without any pretensions. It is not far from the Porta di Nocera.

Tourist Information
Pompeii Town
Via Sacra 1, Cap 80045, tel: 081-850 7255, fax: 081-863 2401.
Pompeii Scavi, Piazza Esedra 2.
Numero Verde, tel: 800-13350 (*see* page 51).

5
The Islands

Italy is blessedly fortunate in the number and variety of its islands, from the exotic Borromean Isles in Lake Maggiore to Stromboli off Sicily and Murano and Burano ghostly in the misty Venetian lagoon, they are many and magnificent. Yet perhaps the most famous are the isles lying off the coast of Campania. These three are particularly renowned, and have been since classical times. In love with their beauties, Roman aristocrats staked claims on these rocky retreats, set like green, white and gold gems in a shimmering sea. These early cultured visitors left many relics, so an additional pleasure is the discovery of many antique sites as you explore. For centuries since then, they have been the destination for the artistic, the flamboyant, and the rich. Famed throughout the world, they are Ischia, Prócida and the best known of all, Capri.

You really should not leave Campania without taking the short journey to these exotic spots. The voyage across an aquamarine sea to experience their breathtaking loveliness is in itself a dream. If **Capri** seems too commercial and crowded (which, alas, it often is) then try the larger and equally fascinating **Ischia**, or closer in to Naples and the mainland, the quiet and little-explored charms of **Prócida**. These two islands will indeed give you a better impression of how people live than the much more international Capri. All three islands are easy to get to on fast and frequent ferries and hydrofoils. Once at the quaysides you have a choice of many pleasures from tours or walks, or just sitting at the cafés and watching life go by.

Opposite: *A popular nature walk on Capri takes you to the Natural Arch.*

Below: *Boats and ferries*
dock at the Marina Grande,
a lively harbour on Capri.

CAPRI

If you have wondered why a tiny place like Capri, only
6km (4 miles) long, has always been considered one
of the ultimate holiday settings for sensation seekers,
then all one can say is 'try it'. This is without doubt one of
the most delectable destinations in the Mediterranean, if
not the world. Butting up from azure seas, the small
cliff-walled isle really is alluring. Once attached to the
long craggy arm of the Sorrentine Peninsula, this final
separated piece of the mainland is spectacular, be it views
of beetling cliff, rugged white rocks, limestone caves, tiny
sand beaches, or pretty towns, all framed by a brilliant
sea. It offers so much for romantics as well as hedonistic
sun and sea lovers. Its picturesque settlements have good
restaurants, sun-splashed cafés and lots of smart little
shops set along narrow atmospheric streets. If you want
to do more than just flop on a café chair, bask on a sandy
spit, or swim in a clear warm bay, then go on a boat trip
or take a stroll. Longer walks in the country along well
marked paths will take you around the island and along
the cliffs for a series of splendid views.

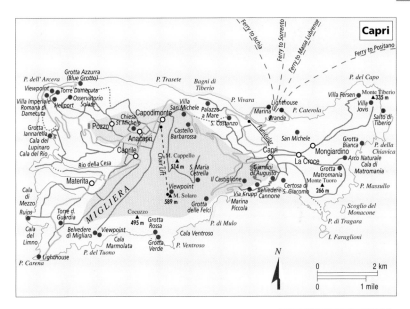

Capri offers a constant kaleidoscope of scenery. Heavenly scents rise from flowers, which are everywhere, or from herbs crushed underfoot. As the afternoon wears on lemons glow in their trees as a big red sun sets over the sea. To visit here is to experience sheer joy.

CAPRI TOWN

Boats dock at the **Marina Grande** on the north side of the island. It's a pretty seaside town, and as the main port and fishing centre, offers good seafood restaurants. From here, it's a steep walk or funicular ride up to the town of **Capri** that spreads itself along the neck of the island, between the two main hills, **Monte Tiberio** and **Monte Solaro**. In the 16th century, with the area troubled by pirates, the town slowly moved back from the sea to the col it now occupies, where the inhabitants could live in relative safety. Capri town centres around the **Piazza Umberto I**, known as the Piazzetta, a square filled with cafés and restaurants, abuzz with chat and social activity from dawn til dusk.

WALKS

Try going on foot in Capri. It is possible to walk on shore-looping paths and up to the heights of Anacapri. Paths are well kept and marked. Strolling at an agreeable pace, you will get your own scenic views, perhaps catch sights of Capri's wildlife, picnic, or pause at a beach for a refreshing swim. Go east to the **Villa Jovis** (Jupiter's Villa), where the entire island can be seen from the terrace. It was here that Tiberius lived, and when enraged, had his victims thrown down the cliff called, **Salto di Tiberio**. Go up to the **Arco Naturale**, to find the imposing palace built on Capri by the Emperor. Allow at least half an hour to climb up from the town.

Above *The Faraglioni are three massive limestone rocks that rise out of the ocean at about 107m (350ft), just off the coast of Capri.*

Things To See

Take a lazy stroll along the narrow, flower-hung passages and alleys of the medieval quarter to the **Certosa di San Giacomo**, a 14th-century Carthusian monastery. Within this simple white church and cloister is a gallery of 17–19th-century paintings. Not far off, the **Belvedere Cannone** sits above glorious views along the cliffs. Below the gardens of the **Giardini di Augusto** offer flowers and shade. The steeply down-dipping **Via Krupp**, plummets down around sharp curves and turns to arrive at the sea and the **Marina Piccola**. Once a fishing village, it now has water sports and beach pleasures.

Capri is indeed enchanting, full of elegant shops and galleries too, but in summer it gets cruelly crowded. Visitors arrive on every boat and the town is completely submerged in a sea of day-trippers. Even so, you can still get away, especially on walks. Or go out of season, stop over in one of the isle's small hotels and you will have quite a different experience.

After you have explored Capri town, head back down to the Marina Grande, and take to the water for a boat tour around the rest of the island. One tour will take you to the dramatic group of rocks south of the island called the **Faraglioni**, but the most sought after is a trip round to the **Grotta Azzurra** (Blue Grotto). This is one of the many flooded caverns found here, but thanks to its extraordinary lighting conditions, it is one of the most spectacular grottoes to be found anywhere. Entered by small rowing boat, it is quite an experience. The craft is propelled by boatmen as it negotiates the narrow entry with its foam and whirl of water. Inside, the enormous high roofed cave presents a sudden calm and the illuminated walls are indeed a ghostly, luminous blue, as light shimmers up in vivid reflections from the pale sand below the water. The visit can be short, but if you are adventurous you can swim in, except wait till the press of boats has decreased as they head home.

Also on Capri are other caverns. At the **Grotta Matromania**, the Romans had a shrine to Cybele. Nearby is the **Arco Naturale**, a huge sea carved stone arch.

ANACAPRI

High up the hill, Anacapri is a pleasing little town, with a detailed scale model of the island in the main square. A bus trip saves you a hard walk (the Scala Fenicia has nearly 800 steps so you need to be energetic). You will be rewarded after the climb with wonderful views to the sea and harbour. Pause, take a refreshing drink, or explore the spectacularly sited Villa San Michele.

In the town centre, the **Church of San Michele** has a majolica pavement of the 18th century representing the Garden of Eden. A few minutes' walk away the simple

> **THE ENGLISH ABROAD**
>
> The English have long loved Capri. Early visitors included 18th-century aristocrats on the **Grand Tour** and as travel grew easier it became more popular with rich visitors in the next century, too. More recently the singer **Gracie Fields** lived here. As a place to let yourself go and have fun it is legendary. **Noël Coward** wrote a comic song about an adventurous woman from London: Mrs. Wentworth-Brewster, a middle class widow freed from London restraints, whose exploits on the Piccolo Marina satirized Capri's swarms of camp-following visitors.

Below: *The Via Krupp on Capri, an impressive road winding its way to the sea.*

Scandinavian design of the Villa San Michele is a stunning contrast to its exotic setting. It was built by Dr. Axel Munthe, a 19th-century Swedish scientist, who wrote a popular book entitled *The Story of San Michele,* about living on the island. As well as the cool, elegant villa itself, he enjoyed creating an enchanting classic Italian garden with spacious loggias and pools. The views of the sea and isle from the pergola perched at the end of the garden above the Scala Fenicia, are amazing. In the house are examples of Italian and Swedish antiques, family mementos and Roman remains found in the gardens.

From the Piazza Vittoria, take a chair lift to the summit of **Monte Solaro,** which at 589m (1930 ft) is the highest point on the island. The views across the entire Bay of Naples are superb. Far below, a small fleet of boats ferries hundreds of tourists around on trips or through narrow cliff openings to visit the Grottoes.

Below: *Take a chairlift up to Monte Solaro, and admire the magnificent views of Anacapri, the only other town on the island.*

ISCHIA

Although Capri is famous there are those who prefer a less renowned place, and find Ischia best of the trio of alluring islands. To begin with there is more space. At 70 km² (27sq miles), Ischia is the largest of the three, furthest out to sea, and opposite Capri. It may be less famous and less visited than the idyllic island of Capri (although very popular amongst the Germans), but Ischia is not second rate. It is a place for the discerning, deserving a special trip, as its scenery is beautifully varied, and its coast cut with creeks and bays. Formed by volcanic eruptions, you are often reminded that its fiery origins took place not so long ago, for there are hot springs everywhere. Its central volcanic

mountains stand out against the serene sky, and from beneath these ancient peaks the thermal springs leap up, their super-heated water forced from deep, underground boilers. There are establishments that provide bathing cures wherever these sulphurous springs pop up, or as they run down to sandy beaches. Unfortunately this island that the Romans loved became a mass market destination some time ago, but this hasn't yet obliterated Ischia's charm.

There are many small quaint villages. The main town is **Ischia Porto**, which is also the ferry port, an old volcanic crater. With neighbouring **Ischia Ponte** this pleasant town has good sandy beaches. There are many facilities where people can try its radioactive volcanic springs. Indeed a substantial number of visitors come to try cures for sufferers of a host of varied ailments. Ischia Ponte, is actually older and named after a dyke connecting it to an imposing fort, the photogenic and part ruined **Castello Aragonese**. This short causeway conducts you to the one-time Aragonese stronghold on its small islet, surrounded by pinewoods and churches.

The presence of hot springs is a major lure for visitors to Ischia's other coastal resort towns. These include **Casamicciola Terme**, **Spiaggia di Citara** and **Sant'Angelo**, possessing springs, beaches, large hotels and a lot of commercial holiday attractions. **Forio** in particular strives to add its own appeal with historic features from small churches to frowning town walls. For those interested in the island's history, nearby **Lacco Ameno** of Greek origin, has a museum of archaeology within the **Villa Arbusto**, an 18th-century

Above: *The enchanting Villa San Michele, Capri.*

WALTON'S RETREAT

For many years, the composer **William Walton**, perhaps best known for his music for films, lived a quiet life here. Knighted for his music, he chose **Ischia** as his retreat. Since the Grand Tour, many wealthy English settlers and amateur gardeners lived in Italy, attracted partly by the warmth, flowers and exotic shrubs. He and Lady Walton created a charming garden here that can be visited. You can also stay here.

Ischia

mansion. Sant'Angelo, benefits in picturesque aspects from its position on a narrow isthmus and tiny isle. It is set in the southern part with steep hills falling to the shore. There are more thermal springs to be found at **Terme Cavascura**, and an impressive natural steam vent, the Fumarole, voids here. From Fontana, a short distance away, it is a stiff hour-long walk up to the summit of the island's highest mountain, **Monte Epomeo** at 788m (2585ft), from where there are vast panoramic views. If you don't want to get footsore you can ride up the mountain on donkeys.

PRÓCIDA

Less visited than Ischia, and often overlooked, take time for a day trip to little Prócida, which is a fascinating place and still relatively unspoilt. You may be quite charmed by it, however, so don't restrict your visit. It is appealing to walkers too, with a chance to spot animal, bird and insect life along its paths and lanes. Lying beside Prócida, a narrow fingernail of land linked by a bridge, takes you to the **Isolotto di Vivara**. You will need to apply to visit this nature-reserve.

Prócida is quite tiny at 4km (2.5 miles) long. It is an island of ancient volcanic origin, with its once high craters long smoothed and broken down by erosion. This intriguing yet simple island offers the visitor that rare thing, a part of Campania that is not over-run with tourists. Like Ischia, it is part of the Campi Flegrei, created in the Tertiary era on a volcanic extension, and seated on ancient lava flows. Along with being the

---

SUNSETS OVER THE SEA

The islands found in the **Bay of Naples** offer a dream combination. Here you get a great array of views, from spectacular settings of rocks, capes, and cliffs to charming little towns pinned onto hillsides and almost tumbling down to the sea. All of these settings are often bathed in the most glorious sunsets. Dramatic views here were imaginatively captured in the past by painters. Now your camera can record some of these most romantic images of Campania.

smallest, it is least developed of the three islands. It is blessedly much freer of the allure of tourist money, so expect simplicity. As you move around you will note a more prosperous past as reflected in its many old crumbling villas. Its present day houses are bright and charming, white or colour-washed and often domed, connected with arcades, terraces, and outdoor stair-cases. They are still lived in for the most part by fisher families, gardeners and wine growers. (Ask to try local wines at cafés or bars.) Everywhere Prócida presents a simple, older lifestyle, its quiet aspect marking it as a charming and as yet undiscovered place.

Chiaiolella, at the end of the island, has good beaches. They are reached past painted houses with terraced gardens, through colourful fishing villages with their boats and cottages set against vines, citrus and olive trees. Here you can feel like a local as you sit in the sun, or swim from uncrowded beaches and eat on the terraces of simple trattoria. Regular ferries dock at the main town of **Marina di Sancio Cattolico** (commonly called the Marina Grande) with its narrow streets that plunge down from the 16th-century **Castello**. Like so many fortified castles in Italy, this was until recently, used as a prison. Stroll through the **Terra Murata** (Walled Town). Also at Terra Murata, is the charming **Certosa di San Michele Arcangelo** (Monastery of the Archangel Michael), its principal treasure, a painting from the Nea-politan School. Luca Giordano was one of Caravaggio's more original pupils. This picture is of the arch-angel, supposedly pre-venting the invasion of Prócida from the Turks.

> **NATIVE FOODS**
>
> As an island of fisherman, Prócida is a great place to try fish. Dishes to look for are those using squid, octopus and shellfish. *Spaghetti alle vongole* (clams) is notable, and mussels steamed or with hot sauce (*zuppa di cozze*), is delicious. Eat them with hunks of local bread, perhaps dipped in olive oil, follow up with flaky pastries using candied peel and ricotta.

Below: *Lemon trees in Prócida. The over-whelming scent of lemons pervades the entire Bay of Naples – they grow everywhere and are used for everything from per-fume to the local speciality liqueur, limoncello.*

The Islands at a Glance

The lure of Capri and the islands is the almost constant **mild weather** in the Bay of Naples. It is rarely cold or dank, although you may expect occasional rain in **spring** and **autumn**. Even in **winter** the sun shines; although it's too cool to sunbathe it is frost free, so the foliage and flowers continue. It is pleasingly warm in spring and autumn. Very busy in the **hot summer** months, however.

Capri offers lovely **walks**, and Ischia, though less compact, also has well marked paths. The views from special points along the routes are splendid. To get around short island distances, **taxis** are much in evidence. Local **bus** lines also ascend the hills and make fairly frequent connections. Bus tickets can be purchased from newsagents; take detailed maps if you are hiking. The islands are connected by **ferry boats** (and some hydrofoils) There are frequent sailings between islands and to Naples.

On Capri
LUXURY

Villa Brunella, Via Tragara 24, tel: 081-837 0122, fax: 081-837 0430, or e-mail: brunella@mbox.caprinet.it
If you prefer the comforts of a modern hotel, built on a steeply terraced slope among the lemon groves, and don't mind lots of steps, this is a great place. The hotel has 20 rooms, sea views and a swimming pool. Seasonal opening.
La Scalatinatella, Via Tragara 10, Capri 80073, tel: 081-837 0633, fax: 081-837 8291. This smart little place is made up of two villas containing, of all things, an array of oriental furniture. All 20 bedrooms are suites, and have jacuzzis and ornate balconies with views. Have lunch by the pool and sop up the atmosphere as well as the succulent food.
Grand Hotel Quisisana, Via Camarelle 2, Capri, 80073, tel: 081-837 0788, fax: 081-837 6080. This is without doubt a place for those with bottomless resources – very expensive and very luxurious it has two top class restaurants and the most marvellous views. It is hard to believe that this large ochre coloured hotel was actually a sanitorium when it first opened in the 1840s.

MID-RANGE

Villa Sarah, Via Tiberio 3/A, tel: 081-837 7817, fax: 081-837 7215. Just outside Capri Town, this 20 room hotel stands in vineyards. Gardens surround the peaceful white painted house. Seasonal opening.

BUDGET

Villa Krupp, Via Matteoti 12, tel: 081-837 0362, fax: 081-837 6489. On the cliff with a view down to the Marina Piccola, this is an historic villa. Both Lenin and Gorki made it their home – tho' not as a couple! There are 12 rooms and a simple air at this quaint family run place. Seasonal opening.
Pensione Quattro Stagione, Via Marina Piccola 1, 80073, tel: 081-837 0041. It may sound expensive being called The Four Seasons, but it is actually a charming little pensione – or as near as Capri gets to one. There are 12 rooms, a pretty terrace, and views. Dinner is available if you book ahead and it is definitely worth trying.

Ischia
LUXURY

Mezzatorre, Località San Montano Nord Forio, tel: 081-986 111, fax: 081-986 015. Not a monastery this time, but a Saracen tower which was once home to Luigi Visconti, the film director. The hotel is built around the old fortification among pines at the northern end of San Montano Bay, just two miles from Forio. A terrace, seawater pool, spa and gardens. Seasonal opening.

MID-RANGE

Il Monastero, Castello Aragonese Ischia Ponte, tel: 081-992 435. Simple and plain rooms in a converted monastery. Situated within

The Islands at a Glance

castle walls and with great views, makes this hotel more than just a bargain.

La Villarosa, Via Giacinto Gigante 5, Ischia Porto, tel: 081-991 316, fax: 081-992 425. If you want to stay right in the centre of town, this 37-room hotel is a good choice. Luxury at a reasonable price with 19th-century antiquities and charm. Open April to October, it also has a swimming pool within its pleasant gardens.

WHERE TO EAT

Capri
LUXURY

Da Paolino, Via Palazzo a Mare 11 Marina Grande, tel: 081-837 6102. Set amidst groves of citrus fruits, this is a charming and popular place to eat. Specialities are grilled local fish and desserts.

Le Canzone del Mare, Via Marina Piccola 93, Marina Piccola, tel: 081-837 0104. Quite a grand place this, and much enjoyed by well-off locals, as well as rich settlers. There is a terrace where you can sit and have a drink, and the food is excellent.

MID-RANGE
Addo Riccio, Via Gradula 4, Grotta Azzurra, Tel: 081-837 1380. Often crowded as it is below the cliff with the entrance to the fabled Blue Grotto nearby. There is an open air terrace with sea views. Dinner only.

Aurora, Via Fuorlovado 18, tel: 081-837 0181. One of those places wallpapered with pictures of celebrities who may have dropped by. A justifiably popular and long-established pizzeria. Closed winters.

Da Gemma, Via Madre Serafina, tel: 081-837 0461. Could appear rather old style and maybe a bit kitsch yet this is a lovely, friendly trattoria. If you don't like the copper pans and pottery, enjoy the very good pasta and pizza. Open all year.

Ischia
LUXURY

Damiano, Via Nuova Circumvallazione Ischia Porto, tel: 081-983 032. Beautiful views of the old port from here, you are high up and can see for miles. The accent is on seafood, and the wines are mostly local or southern. Dinner every evening, except Sundays. Seasonal opening.

MID-RANGE
Da Peppina di Renato, Via Bocca 23, Forio, tel: 081-998 312. Good country food in a trattoria that is charming and friendly. There is an open-air terrace with sea views. The restaurant serves very good seafood. Seasonal opening.

Prócida
Being less of a tourist destination than Capri and Ischia,

there are fewer hotels and Prócida is often considered a mere day excursion from Naples. However you can stay and eat very well on this small compact island.

SHOPPING

The islands have lots of small shops in the town centres offering souvenirs, clothes and local handicrafts. Capri in particular also has fashion boutiques and shops selling luxurg goods and jewellery. Street markets offer bargains in local produce.

TOURS AND EXCURSIONS

Visits to local attractions are all expertly catered for from ancient sites and grottoes with coach and walking guided tours. Check Tourist Offices for many possibilities.

USEFUL CONTACTS

Tourist offices
Capri
Piazza Umberto I, tel: 081-837 0686. Marina Grande Banchina del Porto, tel: 081-837 0634.

Anacapri
Via G. Orlandi 59, tel: 081-837 1524.

Tourist Information
Capri
Head Office, Azienda Autonoma di Cura Soggiorno e Turismo, Piazzetta. Cerio 11, Capri, tel: 081-837 0424, e-mail: touristoffice@capri.it

6
The Sorrento Peninsula

Like a lover from Greek classic tales, the two arms of the Bay of Naples embrace the Mediterranean Sea. They extend from the city around the blue of the bay to form a naturally protected harbour. While the northern arm, stretching from Pozzuoli to Ischia and Prócida, is the result of volcanic action, the southern is mainly limestone, its white and grey rocks marking one of the few non-volcanic areas around the bay. This is the spectacularly beautiful and renowned **Peninsula Sorrentina**, a land mass extending to Capri, which is divided from the mainland by a channel called **Bocca Piccola** at its end. This chapter deals with the north-west facing shore of the peninsula. On the other side is the long Amalfi Drive (*see* Chapter 7).

This extended natural breakwater of rock is moored firmly to the mainland shore. It offers a remarkable tour, with renowned villages clinging to cliffs and hills from Stabio to Sorrento. Drive along over 32km (20 miles) of unparalleled beauty, slowly, for the road loops and dips around the shores and edges a rugged land. There are masses of lovely wild flowers and herbs, rocks cushioned with long lush green grasses, fruitful orange and lemon groves, gnarled olives trees and sweeping draperies of vines. All around is the sea, indescribably blue, clear and brilliant. Hovering like a shadow in the background, ever present against the seductive Italian skies is the all too real Mount Vesuvius, her only flag of possible danger a soft ascending feather of smoke.

Opposite: *Take a pleasant walk around Sorrento, with views of the Bay of Naples.*

THE PASSING OF PLINY

One of the most touching stories of the exploding **Vesuvius** was that of a naturalist, who on hearing news of the eruption, hurried here on a boat to record the eruption and observe it at closer range. It was not a wise decision. The Roman scientist came too close to the clouds of superheated gas, and professional interest resulted in the death of Pliny the Elder by **asphyxiation**.

Below: *The enchanting resort town of Sorrento is packed with tourists in summer owing to its great location and mild climate.*

CASTELLAMMARE DI STABIA

Your trip along the famous peninsula of Sorrento starts south east of Naples at Castellammare di Stabia. This is Italy's main naval base and a thermal resort too; there are no fewer than 28 springs and treatments at the **Antiche Terme**. In classical times it was the spa town of Stabiae and has a very long and varied history going back to the Oscans – who were there even before the Etruscans. Rome took over in the 4th century BC and the town was later rebuilt in an unusual design – a new town of connected houses with villas in the countryside. A neighbour of Pompeii, it too vanished in the great eruption of AD79. The local museum, the Antiquarium, has relics, frescoes, stucco reliefs and sculptures salvaged from Roman buildings of the town. Nearby, several villas that once faced Vesuvius and were buried, have now been excavated. The two-storey **Villa San Marco** had gardens and swimming pools and even today on a visit you can imagine the luxury of the Roman life of the time, along with the well restored **Villa di Arianna**.

They are both about 2km (1 mile) from the present town. The port of Castellammare was revived and repaired in the 18th century and is a working harbour and shipyard today.

You will want to take time to see the spectacular views of sea and rocky shore, but if not there is a faster road to Sorrento by the coast (with some tunnels), from Naples, avoiding Castellammare. The S269, running from the edges of Castellammare is an adventurous trip, however. The drive up the upper slopes of **Monte Faito** offers wonderful vistas, but the road is a cluster of hairpin bends. As you leave the town, turn left to head up Monte

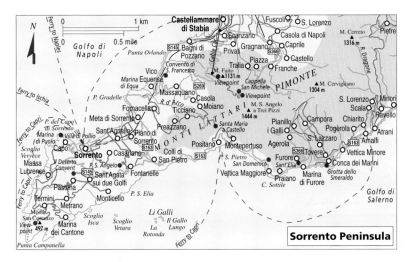

Sorrento Peninsula

Faito, part of the jagged limestone range of the Lattari mountains. This is the high ground that separates the Bay from the Gulf of Salerno. (If you have no car, then take the cable car from Castellammare station up the mountain for an overall view). The road loops and dips dramatically to hit the height and then narrows down to **Vico Equense** through woods. On the way you should stop at several viewpoints for wide panoramas of the Bay of Naples. **Vico**, on the mouth of the River d'Arco, is a small health resort in a pretty rocky setting.

You will also see many vine terraces. For protection against frost, citrus trees are masked with matting in winter, their tender shoots sheltered beneath the covered vine trellises. The drive is most memorable in spring, when many of Italy's wild flowers are in bloom, adding a seductive beauty, while budding new leaves of herbs scent the warm air. On warm days you can also hear the beautiful sounds of birds singing and insects calling.

SORRENTO

Next along this lovely shore comes Sorrento, overlooking its Gulf with views across an azure and violet sea to Capri. Rightly famed as a remarkable resort, it is a perfect

---

VIEWS AND MORE VIEWS

Along the steep mountain road there are several places to stop – with parking. The first you arrive at is **Belvedere del Capi** with a wide view of the Bay of Naples. Further up you come to **Cappella San Michele** with an even wider panorama. The contrast between the mountain scenery and the view below is marked. The climb up is heavily wooded, with many fine beech trees from which the mountain takes its name.

Above: *The Hotel Excelsior Vittoria, offers stunning rooms and views.*
Opposite: *The Piazza Tasso, situated in the centre of Sorrento.*

POETIC HERO

The Piazza Tasso was named after the poet, **Torquato Tasso**, who was born in Sorrento in 1544. He travelled several times to the glittering court of Ferrara to court fame, and elsewhere in the north to enjoy the support of the cultivated Este family. There, he wrote the epic poem for which he is most famous, **Gerusalleme Liberata**, in which Jerusalem is won by Christians. Threaded through the poem is the love story of Rinaldo and Armida. See the statue of Tasso on the square.

---

place to indulge yourself, to stay or just stop and eat, even if you are only passing through. As the principal town of the peninsula ranged along its clifftop, with terraces and ledges, and a scattering of lovely gardens, this resort town has been a place people have come to visit for the last 2500 years. It preserves an air of another era and it is easy to picture late 19th-century visitors playing croquet, or demurely using bathing machines in the sea below, where now modern swimming quays stick out like decks. Sorrento has remained a lovely, stylish, and grand, if somewhat faded place. Despite its popularity, the town has not succumbed to too much commercial adjustment and remains a year-round resort with sophisticated facilities for tourists. Visitors will find a town that is elegant, well-organized and a centre for road, rail and boat connections. It has hotels, inns and many pensiones not to mention cafés, bars and excellent restaurants where you can often eat on terraces to enjoy the warm air. The foliage framing the town is rich and varied from the dark leaves and brilliant gold fruits of the many citrus groves, to exotic shrubs, while colourful flowers embower many houses. Even winter can hardly dull this glorious display.

Sorrento has but one museum, the **Museo Correale di Terranova**. This pretty 17th-century villa houses an old fashioned jumble of all sorts of things, from statuary to a notable collection of 17th–18th-century furniture, china and glass. There are mementos of the town's poet, Tasso, and a terrace with fine views.

This long narrow town is best for sauntering through streets and passages enjoying the wide range of local life at restaurants and cafés spilling onto the pavements. At the foot of the town the old fishing port, the **Marina Grande**, is lively too, while the ferry port in the **Marina Piccola** provides many connections to Naples, Capri, Ischia and several other coastal towns.

Directly above the ferry dock is the centre of the town and the **Piazza Tasso**, honouring Sorrento's 16th-century poet. Along **Corso Italia** you can explore the 18th-century **Palazzo Correale**, with a fine majolica courtyard, and go into the 15th-century **Duomo** (cathedral). Of the other churches, look for the tall belfry of the most interesting, the **Chiesa di San Francesco** (Church of St Francis). It appears Baroque but explore further, for later additions hide a pretty cloister with intertwined stone arches, its charming capitals carved with leaves, in a 13th-century Sicilian-Arabic style.

STAYING IN SPLENDOUR

Sorrento possesses some **lavish hotels** in Belle Epoque style. They exude an elegance and a sophistication that is second to none. Italy's luxurious top hotels, or *grandi alberghi*, offer the best service in the world, whatever the Swiss may say! The **food** often uses local products, for example sauces are heightened and made piquant with the juice of local lemons.

MARQUETRY

Among other local handi-works there is a long-lived local trade in the making of **marquetry**, or **intarsia** works. These objects of intricately inlaid woods, some of them rare and precious, come in many forms, from boxes and trays to quite large pieces of furniture and elaborate pictures. Whether they appeal or not, they are yet another facet of that ever-inventive Italian flair for clever artistry in amazingly detailed works.

Below: *There are dozens of shops selling crafts such as marquetry or intarsia. Try to see these local wood inlay items.*

Touring the Villages

A long walk can encompass several of the pretty villages in the rocky countryside around the town. You will find some settlements such as **Sant'Agnello** and **Meta di Sorrento**, home to the 18th-century Bourbon shipyards, very close by and effectively now residential suburbs. Or if you are up to a long walk and frequent climbs, around 32km (20 miles), follow the car route. You can do half of it around **Pico Sant'Angelo** by ascending the S145 over the hills and heading down towards the Amalfi Coast and Sant'Agata. Standing high on the ridge of the Lattari mountains, which form the backbone of the peninsula, **Sant'Agata sui due Golfi** has superb views to the north and south, over two gulfs, as its name suggests. One is the Bay of Naples, and in the other direction, over the Amalfi Coast you see the Bay of Salerno. On the way back pass through **Colli di San Pietro** then up towards **Piano di Sorrento**, which has a thriving market on Monday mornings. **Meta** has a noteworthy church, the **Basilica Santa Maria del Lauro**. For a real hike head from Sorrento towards the far end of the Penisola Sorrentina where you will find in high, dry hills, with

exotic plants and cacti, a scattering of about 30 small hamlets known collectively as the **Massa Lubrense**. They are well hidden amongst breathtakingly lovely scenery with excellent walks and superb views of the Bay across to Capri.

Circular Drive

The road that circles the end of the peninsula, the S145, traverses a marvel of scenery with wooded hillside views and is a short distance, but can take much longer if you have the time. You can amble along slowly and easily spend a day, taking many pauses and perhaps even having a picnic on the heights. (As already noted, it should be walked by those who have brought the right footwear and clothes, for the hills are quite steep.) A winding road bisects the route across the loop of the shore-hugging S145, so it can be shortened. Start westwards from Sorrento on the S145. At the high point of the cliffy shoreline, **Capo di Sorrento** should be visited – a road conducts you to the headland. At the village of Capo beside the church, you will have to walk, so allow time. You will be rewarded with a thrilling view back to Sorrento.

Continue down the peninsula to Massa Lubrense and the final height of the tongue of land, **Monte San Costanzo**. The south facing shore offers visits to **Marina dei Cantone** on the sea and **Sant'Agata**. The road dips steeply to **Colli di San Pietro**. Return on the S163, which offers wonderful views to the Bay of Naples on its descent before you arrive back in Sorrento.

Above: *In the Baroque church of San Francesco are the 14th-century cloisters, where music concerts are held all year.*

ARTISTIC INSPIRATION

The coast has always attracted **painters** of all sorts and you will often see artists at work intent on capturing the ravishing scenes. There are small **galleries** too, showing images of this area in all sorts of media. Of course you can buy if you feel so inclined, and an original picture makes a good souvenir, but take time when making a selection.

Sorrento at a Glance

Best Times To Visit

Sorrento is a year-round destination with lovely warm weather during **spring** and **autumn**. Like much of this part of the coast, it can get very crowded in **summer**. It is popular with people escaping northern chills in **winter**, when it is mild and frost-free here.

Getting There

The best and most attractive way to get to Sorrento is by **boat**, and the town has a lively port with a well-ordered system of sailing. Sorrento is connected by several **ferries** to nearby ports and Naples – for all port information, tel: 081-807 3071, LMP Ferries, tel: 081-552 2838. If travelling by **bus** from Naples, and once in Sorrento, try the blue SITA buses which run to nearby villages, as well as to Positano and Amalfi. The buses leave from the station. Tickets can be bought from newsagents. There are direct coach services to and from Rome. For **air** connections Autolinee Curreri Service operate a direct bus service to Capodichino Airport four times daily, leaving from Piazza Tasso. For information, tel: 081-801 5420. If travelling by **train**, Sorrento is on the Circumvesuviana line, which includes stops at Pompeii, Ercolano and Naples. When returning, check that you are on the Sorrento section as the line forks. For

information and times, tel: 081-772 2444.

Getting Around

It is an easy town to **walk** but **taxis** are not a problem, tel Sorrento: 081-878 2204 or Sant 1 Agnello: 081-878 1428. The Syrenbus (tel: 081-807 4220) is a **limousine** service for transfers and sightseeing. Local orange **buses**, operated by Severzio Autolinee, serve the town, including the Marina Grande, Marina Piccola, the station and Piazza Tasso en route.

Where to Stay

Plenty of hotels are scattered along the Sorrentine Coast and in Sorrento itself. There are good hotels in other towns, too. Country hotels are also a possibility – for example **Massa Lubrense**, with places offering many amenities as well as gardens and views.

Luxury

Bellevue Syrene, Piazza della Vittoria 5, tel: 081-878 1024, fax: 081-878 3963. Old, grand clifftop hotel built in 1750, and once favoured by parvenu empress Eugénie in the opulent 19th century. Grandiose décors with antiques, paintings and a Pompeiian restaurant. Nice gardens and terraces.
Grand Hotel Excelsior Vittoria, Piazza T. Tasso 34, tel: 081-807 1044, fax: 081-877 1206 or

e-mail: exvitt@exvitt.it
website: www.exvitt.it
Central and imposing, the Excelsior Vittoria, opened in 1834 and is still owned by the same family. It has had many famous guests in its time. Romantic decorations include frescoes and ceramics. Beautiful terrace atop the cliff, and the gardens are alluring. Lift down to the port, pool and restaurant.
Grand Hotel Cocumella, Via Cocumella 7, Sant 1 Agnello, tel: 081-878 2933, fax: 081-878 3712. Just outside Sorrento (3km/2 miles), the oddly named Cocumella is another of those converted monasteries. It is very grand, expensive and exclusive, with gardens and a private beach.

Mid-range

Royal, Via Correale 42, tel: 081-807 3434, fax: 081-877 2905, or e-mail: ghroyal@ maniellohotels.it Yet another old and charming clifftop hotel, maybe less well placed, but still a lovely spot and within range of normal pockets. There are views of Vesuvius from terraces, a pool and gardens. Other hotels in the area under the same management are the Ambasciatori, Capodimonte and Hotel de la Ville.
Villa di Sorrento, Piazza Tasso, tel: 081-878 1068, fax: 081-807 2679. Centrally placed in town, this small hotel offers no views, and

Sorrento at a Glance

plain yet perfectly satisfactory rooms – a very attractive medium price option.

BUDGET

Hotel Loreley et Londres, Via Califano 12, tel: 081-807 3187, fax: 081-532 9001. Also on a clifftop perch, yet this old one-time mansion is now a simple but well appointed hotel with a pool and a warm welcome.

Youth Hostels Association, Salita della Grotto 23, tel: 081-761 2346.

Youth Hostel, Via degli Aranci 60, tel: 081-807 2925.

Outside Sorrento

La Badia, Via Nastro Verde 8, tel: 081-878 1154, fax: 081-807 4159. A real find, this delightful hotel is a converted abbey, set amidst olive and lemon groves on the hill just above Sorrento (on the bus route to the centre; 10 mins), with superb views over the town and bay. Attractively furnished, friendly, with a pool and restaurant.

Capo la Gala, Vico Equense. Via Luigi Serio 7, Capo la Gala, 80069, tel: 081-801 5758, fax 081-879 8747. This near-hidden, modern, 18-room hotel has a series of terraces down the cliff-face. Also has a pool. Economic aspect in the rooms, but a welcoming air.

Hotel Maria, 8001 Massa Lubrense Costiera Sorrentina, tel: 081-878 9163, fax: 081-878 9411. Nice little hotel

just west of Sorrento, on the coast with great views. Restaurant, pool, garden, free shuttle bus to Sorrento. There are 35 rooms with balconies, sea views.

WHERE TO EAT

Sorrento

La Fenice, Via degli Aranci 11, tel: 081-878 1652. The name echoes the opera house that was burned down in Venice. This is one of the best restaurants in town, glassed in, flower-framed. Unusual dishes on the big menus with an accent on local and traditional dishes from Neapolitan pizza to pasta.

Lanterna Mare, Via Marina Grande 44, tel: 081-807 3033. As its name suggests, it is a seafood place with views over the quay and the Marina Grande. A very romantic spot. Elegant service, delicious food, great desserts. Try the same family owned **La Lanterna** situated in town at Via S. Cesareo 23/25, tel: 081-878 1355.

Trattoria da Emilia, Via Marina Grande 62, tel: 081-807 2720. Family run, small yet has a well-cooked range of fish and pasta. It's popular as an authentic family-run trattoria by the sea, with the old-style checked cloths and candles in bottles.

CLUBS AND BARS

Bar Primavera, Via Fuorimuro 20/Corso, Italia 142, tel:

081-878 3375/807 3252.
Circolo dei Forestieri (Foreigners' Club), Via L. De Maio 35, tel: 081-877 3263.
Blu Blu, Internet Café, Via Fuorimura 20/D, tel: 081-807 4854.

SHOPPING

There are numerous small shops selling luxury items in the town, specializing in clothes, leather, linens, shoes, pottery and local handicrafts. Check the local streetmarkets, too. Shop owners almost always speak English; although sizes are in centimetres you will usually find conversion tables are on hand for measurements.

TOURS AND EXCURSIONS

Syrenbus (tel: 081-807 4220), a limousine service offering transfers. Full and half day sightseeing. The rail service offers lovely views, too.

USEFUL CONTACTS

Tourist Offices
Sorrento
Circolo dei Forestieri (Foreigners 1 Club), Via L. De Maio 35, tel: 081-807 4033, fax: 081-877 3397
Guide Centre, Via degli Aranci 187, Sorrento, tel: 081-878 3061/877 2197, fax: 081-877 2197.
Vico Equense, Via San Ciro 16, tel: 081-879 8826, or 801 6146.
Castellammare di Stabia, Piazza Matteotti 34, tel: 081-871 1334.

7
The Amalfi Drive

This is undoubtedly one of the most famous of all scenes, the Costa Amalfitana (Amalfi Coast). Get ready for a treat and a slow drive, speeding is definitely not recommended. Try to avoid weekends too, for many local people are doing the drive themselves then. This relatively short 80km (50 mile) stretch of strand is claimed to be the most beautiful coast in Italy. The impressive corniche style road ripples and turns, flips up and down as it hugs the shore southwest from Salerno, along coves, cliffs, beaches, groves and rocky inland heights all the way along the south coast of the Sorrentine peninsula. It constantly surprises. There is a kaleidoscope of changing views of land and sea. Revealed is a wildly varied and lush landscape against a serene drop of contrasting blues, the sea and the sky. It also shines with a necklace of historic towns.

These ancient little settlements use their very limited space, often a sheer cliff drop to the sea, with incredible ingenuity. You will be surprised at the way tiny towns can pack themselves into these tight steep spaces, offering room along its narrow, often stepped, streets only for the foot walker and maybe barrows, bikes and carts. Below are the always necessary fishing harbours, complete with beached or bobbing boats. You will also get a glimpse of Saracen watch towers, tiny churches, white and colour washed houses, rampant with pretty flowers standing along layers of narrow terraces. There are also beautiful gardens filled with vegetables, and backed with vines, olive, almond and lemon trees.

Don't Miss

*** The Amalfi Coast: one of the world's loveliest stretches of sea coast, with natural scenery and local architecture.
*** Amalfi: offers both charm and history in a ravishing setting.
*** Ravello: a complete hill town with two lovely gardens.
** Positano: a little resort town in a dramatic setting – cliffs and whitewashed houses overlooking the sea.
* The Grotta dello Smeraldo: the Emerald Grotto with similar reflected lighting effects to the Blue Grotto on Capri, but brilliant green.

Opposite: *The charming town of Positano descends the cliff in steep steps.*

HOMAGE TO WAGNER

The German composer, **Wagner** came to Ravello when living in Southern Italy in 1880. An important international Wagner Festival is now held here each July, in the grounds of the **Villa Rufolo**. It still attracts Wagnerians to hear their hero's music among gardens that are the model for Klingsor in his grandiose opera.

Below: *The lush gardens in the Villa Rufolo in Ravello, are a profusion of colour, and present panoramic views.*

RAVELLO

The entry point to the drive is the town of Salerno, reached from the A3 toll road to Pompeii and Naples. Turn at the sign for Vietri sul Mari for the S163, the beginning of the Amalfi Drive in the direction of Ravello. Consider hiring a car for the day to allow you the freedom to stop in parking places and admire the stunning views along the road.

For the kind of visitor who adores Italian charm, the village of Ravello is perfect, an Italian gem in a lovely setting. This scattering of houses along a hill, surrounded by low mountains, which at a colder time of year can be snow swept, presents a lovely prospect from a distance. As so many visitors have found, this is a superlatively lovely place. High on its hilltop over 305m (1000ft) up, it surveys the world, all the way down to Amalfi and the sea, an eagle's eyrie with ledges of gardens, hanging plants and dramatic viewpoints.

Opposite the cathedral, the Norman castle of the **Villa Rufolo** dates to the 11th century although much of it is 13th century in a peculiar mix of Saracen and Norman, only found in Italy. It was the home of the area's most powerful family, a palace for popes, also a king, its Gothic entry leading to a Moorish courtyard with elegant arches in interlaced Sicilian style. This former cloister is dominated with a formidable, if crumbling keep. Writer Boccaccio stayed here and even Wagner loosened his

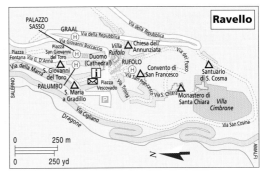

Teutonic crown to be seduced by the beauties of Ravello – he liked it so much he made the garden into a magical setting, in his opera *Parsifal*. The famous gardens with their coastal views do indeed seem an enchanted place.

There is, however, a second Ravello garden that is even more impressive. A short distance from the central piazza, look for a stepped street leading to the twin churches of **San Francesco** (St Francis – pause to view the 13th-century cloister) and **Santa Chiara** (Church of St Clare). Beyond is the **Villa Cimbrone**. Here you find a witty exercise in gardening, opening to lawns and English rose beds, which rarely seem at home in such settings. This lovely garden with its odd cloister (look for the droll little images of the Seven Deadly Sins) and the nymph's grotto, contains a number of arbours, paths and statuary of varied origins. You are then seduced along to the final surprise as cool mossed walks with overhanging foliage end in a wide alley and a belvedere studded with marble busts that presents fabulous views of the hills and the Amalfi coast below.

Ravello's **cathedral** was started in 1086 and as so often happened in Italy, altered in the 18th century as new fashions dictated. Its façade testifies to this. Within, its ancient columns have been uncovered, cleaned and restored. Go inside, for the church is extraordinary for its rich and fantastic interior mosaics, mostly 13th-century. The inlaid marble pulpit by Niccolo di Foggia is a remarkable and dramatic one; an eagle soars above it and it is perched in Northern Italian Romanesque style on sculpted lions. In its mosaics the animals are lively, and equally splendid is a second smaller monument, an ambo with more mosaics of Jonah and the Whale, mostly in green. Look at the 12th-century

---

ENGLISH GARDENER

It was in the late 19th century that **Lord Grimthorpe**, acquired and remodelled the Villa Cimbrone, and it is very much his creation. Here is yet another English aristocrat caught up with the romantic aspects of Italy, living away from home and busy employing his fortune in the creation of a legend. The two boars carved over the entrance make up the Grimthorpe Crest, and the garden's creator himself is buried nearby.

Above: *The Museo dei Corallo (Coral Museum) in Ravello, shows the fine tradition of coral being carefully handcrafted into jewellery and cameos.*

bronze door, by Barisano da Trani. It has 54 sculpted panels of the life of Christ and his saints. In a side chapel the blood of the patron saint of the cathedral, San Pantaleone, is kept, and it is said to liquify miraculously every year. A small museum in the crypt contains additional mosaics and sculpture, including a silver reliquary head.

More antique columns line the little **church of St John**, which was also touched up in the 18th century but frescoes in the crypt and a grand early pulpit survive. There is a cameo shop with examples of cameos and coral. If you are robust and it isn't too hot you can try your legs on the climbing pathways, for most of the town is inaccessible to motorized transport.

A lovely time to walk around the town of covered passages, flights of steps and tiny alleys is the early morning, or the afternoon, when the upland air is warm and clear, and the views are at their best. Ravello's town centre is small and compact and there are several central hotels to stay at; stylish places with gardens and wide views, their rooms decorated with antiques. There are many possibilities for lunch or dinner on terraces, or in dining rooms – a chance to try the local wines too, so ask wine waiters for advice. They are not fine wines, but well worth sampling, and you should certainly eat in good style.

If you are planning to stay for a few days, Ravello is an excellent choice for a centre of exploration being almost half way along the Amalfi Drive. You will find it an excellent town if you want to simply get away and relax in beautiful settings. In the hotter months the hilltop place is cooler too, and for day outings there are regular bus connections down to Amalfi. You descend from Ravello on a good winding road and cross the Dragon River Valley turning right to pass the village of Atrani and then heading for your next port of call, Amalfi.

AMALFI

Amalfi claims a long and lively history that stretches back to the empire of Byzantium. Supposedly founded by Roman citizens who left Rome to escape invading barbarian hordes, the area began to recover early in the 9th century, and rapidly established itself as the chief town of the coast. With a burgeoning population, Amalfi grew into a leading city and by AD958 was the seat of a duke.

There is lots to do and see here. The 11th-century Duomo cannot to be missed in its theatrical setting at the top of a flight of steps. It could be the opening scene of Cavalleria Rusticana in which the steps are crowded with chanting spectators at the start of the Easter ceremony. The **Duomo di Sant'Andrea** is on Piazza del Duomo. The church was remodelled in the 11th century and the glittering façade, which you approach up a flight of steps, was renovated in the 19th century. The only original part is the campanile with its multi-domed top. Most interesting are the imposing bronze doors, cast in Constantinople in 1065, following a fashion of these parts for massive portals. (The mosaics are much later, but based on the Sicilian-Byzantine original.) If you like Baroque, the interior with its ceiling of wooden inlay will definitely appeal. It's worth searching out the lovely 13th-century **Cloister of Paradise**, with its double columns and a set of interesting

> **SIGHTSEEING IN STYLE**
>
> Although much of the area around Naples is well served by train and bus services, the **Amalfi Drive** itself is less fortunate. It is nicest if you are driven along this road, for even though it is so scenically notable it is also necessary to maintain constant control as it is **narrow**, **twisting** and **cliff hugging**. A driver will really not be able to enjoy it properly so consider asking the hotel to send a car for you. They usually will, though it is not a cheap option.

Below *Lying between cliff and sea, Amalfi town is a splendid place to wander around. The churches and houses are situated above the colourful harbour.*

PAPERMAKING

An ancient craft of fine **paper-making** is still practised here right in the town, and fine water-marked stationery or special paper for painting in watercolour is produced. Dating back to the 11th century, papermaking at the little factory and the paper-mill involves processing the hand-made product all the way from pulp to paper.

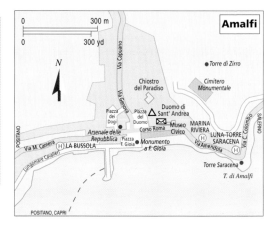

Opposite: *The Duomo di Sant'Andrea dominates the town's main piazza. As you walk up the many stairs, admire the façade, decorated in fine mosaics.*
Below: *The rocky coastline of the Amalfi, overlooking the clear azure sea.*

sarcophagi. Only open at certain hours, the Chiostro del Paradiso combines austerity with Arab decoration. In the crypt are kept relics of the cathedral's patron apostle, St Andrew, filched from Constantinople during the Crusade of 1206. The cathedral also contains a museum of sculptures, pictures and gems.

In its early days of glory, Amalfi was a trading city like Italy's other maritime republics, Venice, Pisa

and Genoa, supplying galleys for the Crusades and plying for goods as far away as Constantinople and the Orient. Amalfi still retains links with the three other Italian maritime cities, now much bigger than this little town, which has long been confined and prevented from sprawl by its restricted site. Amalfi was the first city in the world to codify maritime law and navigation. In the 11th century, the *Tavoli Amalfitane* was proclaimed, regulating all ships using the Mediterranean and establishing laws that were used until the 17th century. This book of maritime laws is now housed in the Town Hall. Amalfi was to become the first of Italy's Maritime Republics in AD840, then soon after it was made a dukedom, and ruled by a doge. Its affluence continued

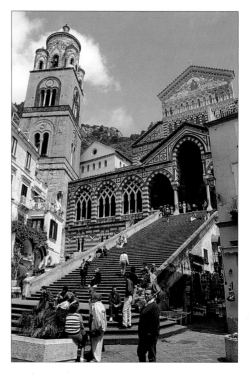

growing well past the 11th century. Amalfi's ships, made in the Republic's arsenal, rode far and wide over the inland sea, and it was crusaders from this tiny place who founded the Knights of St John.

The ranks of white houses of Amalfi rear up against a brilliant sky as you approach the principal town of the coast, most notably from the edge of the sea. Its medieval sea trading brought great riches to the cliff-side town which gave its name to the Amalfi Coast, and this opulent period is reflected today in its monuments and buildings. Now its port is reduced, but as an important and ever-popular resort, Amalfi offers many small attractions as well as major sights. The town has two main streets, **Via Capuano** and **Via Genova**, commencing at the cathedral's piazza. They

---

MARITIME COMPETITION

Venice, Genoa, Pisa and Amalfi partake in an **annual regatta**. Although Amalfi is the smallest of the ancient maritime republics, and has a very limited harbour space, it still manages to hold the annual regatta, which alternates among the four. A set of special costumes is kept in the town hall just for this event. The duomo is dedicated to Saint Andrew, patron saint of sailors everywhere.

are both lined with shops and cafés, galleries and studios. Balconies lean out over the streets, and striking up and down off the two streets are small passages worth exploring, as they very often lead to lovely, tiny gardens and piazzas with fountains. Look for the **Piazza Flavio Gioia**, named for the local man who, supposedly, invented or perhaps just perfected, the mariner's compass. He is certainly looking at a compass in the statue standing before the Town Hall.

In this ancient little city and its satellite towns, even the hotels are very special and often in the oldest and most surprising buildings, ranging from palaces to religious foundations. Though it has to be said facilities are completely modern even if the furnishings are often antique. The **Cappucino Convento** in Amalfi, which is now a grand hotel, sits on a high point reached by an elevator up the cliff. A lovely place to sit and admire the view from under grape arbours, or from the garden terraces. The **Luna Convent**, also a hotel at present, is original too – maybe St Francis wasn't as ascetic as history claims, for he certainly found a fine place to perch his establishment. Some 12th-century buildings remain, a cloister too, all adding to the charm of this hotel within a Saracen tower and a medieval monastery. A short walk up from the cathedral, it's still owned and managed by the same family. They have been here since 1825 and it's certainly the oldest hotel in town. There is a swimming pool, gardens,

---

INSIDE AN EMERALD

The strange Grotta dello Smeraldo, not far from Amalfi, is a flooded sea cavern infused with eerie reflected light of a brilliant emerald green. The cavern floor has been altered due to earth movements and there are underwater stalactites and a bizarre submerged crib. The Smeraldo Grotto is accessible by an elevator, or stairs down from the road or by sea.

and sea views. They are very proud of the fact that the peripatetic Henrik Ibsen wrote one of his masterpieces, 'A Doll's House' here.

POSITANO

Positano was part of the Amalfi Republic in the 9th–11th centuries; and again in the 16th–17th centuries, when it was a trading centre which actually rivalled bigger maritime cities in Italy. Positano has always been popular as a resort, in spite of its extraordinary terrain. It has a virtually vertical aspect, for the little town tumbles in terraces, paths, passages and flights of steps down a steep slope towards the sea. Take special care on wet days. The town itself is alluring, with fishermen's dwellings piled alongside grand villas above a small sandy beach lined with painted fishing boats. You would not think there was a possibility of tucking in another place to eat or stay in such a vertically inclined settlement. Yet there has been

WINTER FESTIVITIES

If you want to see the coast in an unusual and dramatic light, come at **Christmas** or **New Year**. The weather is usually mild, and there are fireworks all along the sea and street entertainers. Special dishes of the season, such as game, wild boar, and codfish appear on menus.

Opposite: *The narrow streets in Amalfi are lined with appealing boutiques.*
Below: *Positano ends at the sea with the Marina Grande pebble beach, marked with fishing boats.*

SIREN SONG

Off in the sea to the south-west of Positano are the tiny islands known as **Li Galli**. According to legend, these were the islands where **Sirens** supposedly perched, singing their alluring notes to passing sailors to strand Odysseus on the rocks. Certainly the islands, if not the Sirens themselves, attracted Rudolf Nureyev who lived here, when visiting the Amalfi coast.

Below: *Positano's Moorish-style architecture.*

further controlled development of this picturesque town of small whitewashed houses with a Moorish look. It now has a permanent population of about 4000. One road gives vehicular access and, believe it or not, there is a small bus that runs around, though many hotels and apartments have only pedestrian access.

Positano town is special in a direct way, it remains essentially a fishermen's village in spite of the sophisticated visitors who flock here from all over the world, all year round. It retains a sweet compelling charm, pastel-pretty by day and romantic at night with its alluring restaurants under the stars. There really is very little to offer those in search of antiquities or splendid architecture. You might say it just has itself to parade, and that for many is enough when they come to visit this pretty little town, ranged along its ledges and terraces down the sea facing cliff. There is a small and lively harbour, a cathedral and lots of little shops, as well as plenty of places to eat and drink. As a place to say it is unique, however, with its enormous charm and lovely setting of cliff and cove, and inlet. The gardens are as grand as anywhere else on this magical coast, the streets are very steep and often stepped. What Positano does have, is a huge range of places to stay; from the grand to the simple, from the most expensive to the reasonable, and some of them are quite special and beloved by their regular guests. There is the eccentric San Pietro, there are converted villas (the Bucca di Bacco and the Poseidon) and even a one time palace, the Palazzo Murat, once lived in by Napoleon's brother in law, the king of Naples. Believe it or not, there are actually 72 hotels here. Finding staff must be difficult indeed.

SMALLER RESORTS

Do not feel restricted to stay at one of the larger settlements along the drive, for there are many several small resorts to choose from along a coast whose biggest attraction is the splendid **Grotta dello Smeraldo** (Emerald Cave). Visit **Conca dei Marini** with its ruined watch tower, **Marina di Praia,** a small beach surrounded by fishermen's houses, or **Vettica Minore**.

If you want a quiet beach resort for a perch, **Praiano** is an ideal little place. Very quiet, yet close to Positano, it offers a choice of accommodation, and has a picturesque little harbour and a really good beach. For those in search of nightly entertainment there is a disco beside the beach here. At any of the small ports or resorts, there will be good restaurants usually with al fresco terraces and the food is generally delicious, especially the frutta di mare, or crustacea, and pasta with fish.

Easily missed, although just off the main road as you drive to Amalfi, the little fishing port of **Atrani** is well worth a visit. From the piazza explore the narrow stepped streets rising up the steep hill past tiny courtyards and tall white houses, until you find several little restaurants at the top of the town for a welcome pause or a meal. In the town are two notable churches, one, San Salvatore, has a bronze door similar in style to Amalfi's.

Although the route to the mainland from Amalfi is still fascinating, with the vivid sea beside you, and lots of scenic surprises, it is a less exclusive area. Consequently

Above: *One of the many stalls in Positano that display the colourful beach wear that this town is famous for.*

> **STAR TURNS**
>
> Many great artists have lived or worked on this coast. **Boccaccio** made it a setting for a scene in the Decameron (1349–53). In Positano the great Russian maestro, **Sergei Diaghilev,** worked with the Ballets Russes that took Paris and London by storm in the first decades of the 20th century. In his entourage were **Nijinsky, Picasso, Massine** and **Stravinsky**. **Franco Zeffirelli** is the latest international star to claim a toehold here.

Above: *The pastel and white houses and shops are closely packed together in the quiet town of Atrani.*

on the road to Salerno there are interesting, less visited small resorts. These can be well worth a stop off. Not far from Atrani, and on the sea with a small sand beach, is Minori. It's a charming village with a surprise – an ancient site, a 1st-century Roman villa, which can be visited. There are hotels and restaurants in the close-packed streets behind the shady seafront drive. There's a tourist office, too.

If most of the seaside settlements are too quiet and you want a more lively place, try Maiori, a very different sort of resort a little further on. Here there are lots of busy bars and surprisingly good eating places for fish along a long, wide beach. A nice walk, or a local bus takes you on to a real discovery – tiny Cetara.

Vietri sul Mare

A small town at the very beginning of the route, that is not so concerned with lazing by the sea and sunbathing even though it is right on the coast, is Vietri sul Mare near Salerno, at the turn of the major A3 road. This little place with its terraced houses climbing up the slopes of the hills, is devoted to just one thing – the making of fine ceramics. A good place to consider for a visit if the weather turns cloudy or damp – which it can do, even here. In Vietri, you can stroll at a slow pace, from place to place, to compare what is on offer from whole dinner services to solo items, or choose from the many outside stands, which seem to crowd every street. There are several factories, and quite small workshops too, so there is a great deal of choice and a lot to consider before you part with your pennies. It is a good idea to check at the Tourist Office, which is located on Vietri's central piazza, before you wander as they will have information on special exhibitions, master craftsmen and how to visit smaller studios and artists at work. Vietri itself also offers splendid views of the coast, and you can easily combine a day out here with a trip into Salerno, its bigger neighbour.

CETARA

If you prefer a dip in a clear sea from a tiny beach, try Cetara. This fishing village, pressed into its narrow valley, only has one hotel, called the Cerus, with its own private beach.

WELL CONNECTED

Main transport connections can be made from near Vietri, for it is an exit off the A3 autoroute, as is Salerno. This city is connected to the main rail system so you can get fast trains here for Naples, or further on to Rome and the North. In Naples the daily paper lists train and boat departures for the whole area.

Left: *The Norman-Saracen watchtower makes a striking picture for visitors travelling the Amalfi Coast.*

Amalfi Coast at a Glance

The Amalfi Coast has similar weather and temperature conditions to Capri and the islands. Note, however, that the drive itself can become very busy on weekends and during public holidays.

Superb views from your **car** as you follow the famous Amalfi Drive, or you can take sea connections by **ferry** from other resorts, or Naples. Some visitors even take **helicopters** – if you are staying at the San Pietro in Positano!

Amalfi and the Amalfi Coast

LUXURY

Cappuccini Convento, Via Annunziatella 46, tel: 089-871 877, fax: 089-871 886. Very grand old style at this 12th-century convent with wonderful views and a cliff-top terrace. Take the lift up from the main road to this marvellous place. Now a hotel with 77 bedrooms, many have balconies and sea views, antique furnishings and fine décor. Take a stroll before dinner in the terraced gardens. **Luna-Torre Saracena**, Via P Comite 33, tel: 089-871 002, fax: 089-871 333. St Francis suposedly founded this monastery, now an 81-room hotel with views down to the sea. Some of the original 12th-century work and a

cloister can still be seen. The hotel is enclosed within the old monastery and there's a Saracen tower, too. The family who own it, have done so since 1825 – it's Amalfi's oldest. Surrounding this luxurious clifftop place are lovely gardens and a pool. **Santa Caterina**, Strada Statale Amalfitana 9, tel: 089-871 012, fax: 089-871 351. Art Déco is becoming more and more fashionable, and this 99-room seaside hotel reflects the 20s style. It is the best place to stay in Amalfi. There is a seawater pool, but you can also take a lift down to the beach. The hotel offers gardens, lemon trees, fine views, a terrace and even a gym. About 1km (0.5 mile) from Amalfi, along the coast road. There are separate villas.

MID-RANGE

La Bussola, Lungomare dei Cavalieri 1, tel: 089-871 533, fax: 089-871 369. A bit plain yet perfectly comfortable. This old converted mill is family run and has a terrace with good sea views.

BUDGET

Lido Mare, Largo Ducci Piccolomene 9, tel: 089-871 332, fax: 089-871 394. This hotel has a decided Moorish air, with whitewashed walls and arches in North African style. Cool and pleasingly simple; some rooms have sea views.

Positano

LUXURY

San Pietro, Via Laurito 2, tel: 089-875 455, fax: 089-811 449. This very expensive modern hotel is almost hidden in a cliff-side, 1 mile east of Positano. High profile guests, from Princess Diana to film stars, have enjoyed its views and fine food. There's a pool, tennis courts and terraces, a helipad and a private beach. **Palazzo Murat**, Via dei Mulini 23, Positano, tel: 089-875 177, fax: 089-811 419. This is a great little hotel (38 rooms) for those with a taste for history. Napoleon married off his ralations to the aristocracy and Princess Murat was his sister. Stay in her palace – now a smart in-town hotel, yet not too expensive, with a court-yard garden. Closed in winter.

MID-RANGE

Albergo Casa Albertina, Via della Tavolozza 3, tel: 089-875 143, fax: 089-811 540. A rooftop seafood restaurant adds to the appeal of this small and friendly 39-room hotel. In the centre of town, and with views down to the sea. Local crafts on display. **Miramare**, Via Trara Genoino 25-27, Positano, tel: 089-875 002/3, fax: 875-21 929. Many people prefer this nice little hotel with lots of atmosphere to the large and grand. It has 29 rooms, 15 of which have great bathrooms, and the location is dramatic – on a

Amalfi Coast at a Glance

cliff edge above the sea. Wide, perfect views from its terraces.

BUDGET
Maria Luisa, Via Fornillo 40, tel/fax: 089-875 023. A low priced and simple 10-room spot. Very friendly.
Youth Hostel, Via G Marconi 358, tel: 089-875 857.

Ravello
LUXURY
Palumbo, Via San Giovanni del Toro 16, tel: 089-857 244, fax: 089-858 133, or e-mail: palumbo@amalfinet.it
An old Moorish mansion with panoramic views. The Palazzo Confalone, is the setting for this very grandly designed and beautifully decorated hotel. You will be well catered for here. It is expensive, but there is also a cheaper modern annexe.

MID-RANGE
Villa Maria, Via Santa Chiara 2, tel: 089-857 255, fax: 089-857 071. There are two hotels here. The older Villa is next to the modern Giordano, both managed by the same family. Pool, terrace with gardens, 45 rooms, and not far from the centre of town.

BUDGET
Villa Amore, Via dei Fusco, tel/fax: 089-857 135. A 22-room converted villa with gardens and views from its high cliff perch. Nice location near town, simple and friendly.

WHERE TO EAT

Amalfi
La Caravella, Via Matteo Camera 12, tel: 089-871 029. Local seafood is the speciality, as well as superb desserts. Medium-priced, rather plain in looks, but well worth a visit, though you should book ahead. Closed all November.
Trattoria Da Gemma, Via Frà Gerardo Sasso 9, tel: 089-871 345. An old-established, well-loved, local restaurant. There is an open-air terrace and delicious local seafood. It is popular, so try to book in advance. Closed August.

Positano
La Buca di Bacco, Via Rampa Teglia 8, tel: 089-875 699. Medium-priced and good quality Neapolitan dishes. This century-old waterfront bar is still popular, sit outside and eat on warm nights. The name comes from Bacchus, that jovial god of good drinking.
Chez Black, Via Brigantino 19, tel: 089-875 036. Good pasta and pizza here, beside the harbour and beach. Try the seafood pasta and finish your meal with one of their excellent ice creams. Closed during the winter season.

Ravello
Cumpà Cosimo, Via Roma 44-46, tel: 089-857 156. Centrally located, and often crowded trattoria. Big servings. The accent is on their fine pasta dishes.

CLUBS AND BARS

As the Amalfi Coast is an international destination, there are inevitably smart night clubs.
Africana, Via Torre a Mare Praiano, tel: 089-874 042. Very dramatic set in a cave, with a glass dance floor over the sea. This is the smartest of the local night spots. You get to it down a cliff path.
Torre Saracena Amalfi, tel: 089-871 084. Searching for different and exotic settings, the owners have situated this lively late night place in a Saracen tower, just outside the town. Great atmosphere!

SHOPPING

Lots of small places in town have a range of souvenirs (look for local handiwork and crafts), plus luxury goods of all kinds. For a few foreign language newspapers, or books try:
Savo Bonaventura, Via Repubbliche Marinare 17, Amalfi, tel: 089-871 180.

USEFUL CONTACTS

Tourist Offices
Positano
Via Saraceno 1, tel: 089-875 067/875 760.

Amalfi
Corso Roma 19/21, tel: 089-871 107/872 619.

Ravello
Piazza Duomo 10, tel: 089-857 096/857 657.

8
Salerno and Paestum

It is easy to overlook the long coast that runs southeast of the Amalfi Drive. Yet for the more adventurous it has many attractions and historic associations. Beaches and seascapes do predominate, yet there is much to discover inland and once embarked you may want to stay for a time, recognizing that the splendours of the Bay of Naples rather overshadow these simpler attractions. For the adventurous visitor, stretching along the Gulf of Salerno beyond the town of the same name, is a fascinating drive past villages and wide views to the important ancient sites of Paestum and Velia. Further to the south you will find the towns of Agropoli and Pioppi on a sea coast excursion. There are many scenic joys of sea and shore as the road winds on for quite a distance to Palinuro on its point, beside the bewitching Gulf of Policastro. From here the road extends to the border of the neighbouring province of Basilicata.

One of the cities here is a most famous one, founded 250 years ago and recognized as one of the most important discoveries in Italy. It is the large archeological site known as Paestum with its temples and museum. The modern town offers a wide beach shaded by pine woods.

DON'T MISS

*** Paestum:** one of the grandest temples in the world, set in a large archae-ological site that was lost for centuries.
** St Matthew, Duomo Salerno:** although much altered, the Romanesque cathedral has some remark-able features, from huge doors to inlaid pulpits and treasures in its museum.

SALERNO

The first town on the drive south is Salerno. The main road runs right down the front of the town along the shore hugging Lungomare Trieste with its green borders and palm trees. This is an active industrial port, yet still offers much charm, and the extensive views over the Gulf of Salerno from here are very fine.

Opposite: *The Byzantine bronze doors to the Duomo in Salerno, which was built by the Norman leader, Robert Guiscard in 1085.*

Salerno

The town expands to the hillside behind, around a Norman cathedral. There is a castle on its hill above the Gulf and the old part of town stretches below it. Salerno is a busy port and centre for light industries, while small farms and market gardens surround it.

Once a more important city than Naples, the history of Salerno is a long complicated one going back to the Etruscans who founded it. Then came Rome, and after attaining considerable status more than 2000 years ago under the invading Lombards as a principality, Salerno became even more important as the capital city of later invaders from the north – the Normans, under the rule of Robert Guiscard around 1077. Guiscard founded the cathedral, although not much remains of its original state today. The town rose in prominence under the Normans throughout the next two centuries and developed a notable university, but from the arrival of the next invaders, the Angevins, it declined and as a result Naples rose to become the most important centre of the region.

On the 9th of September 1943 Salerno witnessed the invasion of the Allies who were to precipitate Italy's defeat in World War II. American soldiers of the 5th US Army landed south of the town and began the push up the peninsula as part of the offensive that eventually toppled the dictator Mussolini. The area saw much military action as the movement north to Rome began.

Although an important town and capital of its province, Salerno seems just an industrial town and is often bypassed, which is a pity. Within its heart are several interesting sights, notably an extensive medieval

CITY OF SOCRATES

Salerno gained this sobriquet connecting it with the great Greek philosopher when it was at its apogee and had become rich from trading. Its university was soon to be renowned and was well known among the foremost minds of the age, as scholars arrived to work and teach here. Particularly noted for its School of Medicine, it grew quickly under the Normans. Founded in the 11th century its international fame declined after the 13th.

section and the charming Via Mercanti with old shops and houses, one end focused on a very ancient monument, the Arco di Arechi, at its western limit, dating from the Lombard period.

The duomo, the cathedral of St Matthew, has been much changed in the 900 years of its life, yet still retains some spectacular aspects, notably the great 12th-century bronze doors. These were made in Constantinople and of the same date are pulpits, inlaid with mosaics, in similar style to others in Campania. There is a museum attached to the duomo with treasures and architectural relics. There is also a provincial museum here with some fascinating finds from local archaeological digs.

VELIA

Unlike its neighbour, Paestum, not much remains of this city in the province of Cilento. It was an important centre however, and there are extensive ruins. The ancient Elea it was founded in 535BC by Greeks escaping the Persian advance, and the large settlement soon became a prosperous port, later notable for its school of philosophy. Here Zeno became the originator of the Stoic philosophy and later succeeded his master Parmenides, one of the

> **DEADLY PESTS**
>
> Until its origins were known, and draining wetlands became an answer, malaria was a terrible scourge of Italy's low lying marshy districts, from Tuscany to the toe of the boot. It was a major problem here at Paestum, lying near flat soggy fields, haunted by clouds of invading mosquitoes. Carrying the dreaded disease, the ensuing infections eventually decimated the inhabitants so much that even during the Roman Empire the people left. A long process had begun during which the town began slowly to fade away and die.

Below: *A typical street scene in the industrial suburbs of Salerno.*

Above: *About 40km (25 miles) from Salerno lie the ancient Greek ruins of Paestum, believed to have been founded around 600BC.*

best known philosophers before Socrates. Once a base for Brutus after the death of Julius Caesar, Velia declined with the fading of Rome.

PAESTUM

Paestum is an incredible place. This very important antique site was discovered in the mid 18th century during road building. The once great city of the coastal marshes lay hidden for many centuries, submerged under a cover of trees and bushes, now an open dry plain. Its outstanding temples are surprisingly well preserved today, standing in a sylvan setting of fields backed by hills. It was at first a Greek colony founded around 600BC, called Poseidonia. Then after a couple of centuries the city declined and was appropriated by Rome in 273BC. As a dwindling settlement Paestum lingered on into the medieval period, but subject to Saracen offensives and the deadly bite of malarial mosquitoes, it was eventually abandoned.

Now only a cluster of ancient gold and grey stone buildings with extensive fragments of its encircling fortifications, in its great days it must have been a magnificent city with miles of high walls surrounding temples, forum and houses. Here the splendidly simple Doric style is particularly well represented in pale yellow limestone, most notably in the magnificent Temple of Nettuno. Originally settled by Sybarites, who famously gave their name to standards of excessive luxury, the city reflects their elegance in the Tomb of the Diver, only discovered in 1968.

To walk around the ruins you will need plenty of time, so allow at least two hours. Follow the Via Sacra from the entry at the Porta della Giustizia. On the right you will see the Basilica dating from the town's very earliest days with its 50 unusually curved columns, and

---

ANTIQUE SPLENDOUR

The temple of Neptune at Paestum is a marvellously well preserved building of the 5th century BC. This grand and impressive yellow limestone building was thought to have been dedicated to Neptune (or Poseidon in Greek) but later it was discovered that the presiding deity was actually the queen of the gods, Juno (the Greek Hera.) It is a simple and satisfying structure, unadorned and pure containing a three aisled chamber with solid Doric columns supporting triangular pediments and an entablature.

porch dedicated to Hera. Then there is the larger Temple of Neptune, also constructed of limestone, huge and best preserved of all. Next is the Forum with its portico and surrounding shops and just beyond the Ampitheatre (Roman) through which the modern road cuts, and finally the Gymnasium. The rovine, or ruins of ancient dwellings, cluster around these principal buildings and temples.

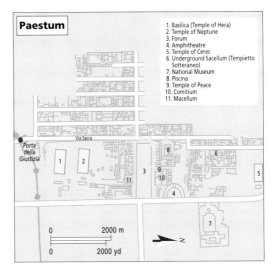

Paestum

1. Basilica (Temple of Hera)
2. Temple of Neptune
3. Forum
4. Amphitheatre
5. Temple of Ceres
6. Underground Sacellum (Tempietto Sotteraneo)
7. National Museum
8. Piscina
9. Temple of Peace
10. Comitium
11. Macellum

Via Sacra

Porta della Giustizia

0   2000 m
0   2000 yd

N

An unusual underground temple follows, (Tempietto Sotteraneo) with a fine collection of bronze vases. The Temple of Ceres is next dateing from the 6th century BC. Originally built in honour of Athena it has columns, some pediments and a sacrificial altar. Visit the Museum which contains Greek funerary murals which may be unique. They were contained within the Tomb of the Diver (Tuffatore), in which the diver is discovered in lively, lightly erotic frescoes. There are sculpted details from the temples here too, and handsome 6th century BC low relief metopes, notably featuring the feats of Hercules, from the sanctuary of Hera about 10km (6 miles) north of Paestum. (There are other elegant metopes on the site.)

You can stay at one of many pleasant hotels in the modern settlement beside the beach, and there are nice restaurants, too, in this pleasant little seaside resort among pine trees.

Below: *The Temple of Neptune was built around 450BC. It is one of the most complete Greek temples in Europe, with only the roof and some of the interior wall missing.*

Salerno and Paestum at a Glance

Any time is good to visit, as like all of the coast, it has a **mild** and agreeable climate. Salerno has some tourist attractions but it is basically a business city with a lively port, much modernized after war damage in 1943 and rather scruffy. It's a useful place to find reasonable accommodation, however, for those who want a base for touring and don't want to spend a lot of money in the smart centres. Paestum does have a busy tourist visiting period from late **spring** to **autumn** with crowded times likely in July and August, when the great temples are popular with all sorts of tour groups. If you can, go out of season and you will see more.

This city is connected to the main rail system so you can get fast **trains** here for Naples, or further on to Rome and the North. There are plenty of trains from Naples to Salerno, and a regular train service from Salerno to Paestum. The station is at the Piazza Vittorio Veneto with local and city bus-stops. There are **bus** services to Naples, Amalfi and Positano, from 119 Corso Garibaldi, the SITA station. Buses for Paestum and places further south leave Piazza della Concordia at the quayside. Paestum is high on tourism lists for organized tours. There are **ferry** and **hydrofoil** services to Amalfi and Positano, almost every hour from the harbour. For up to date timetables you can check the local newspapers. In Naples, the daily paper lists train and boat departures for the whole area. If travelling by car, Salerno is easily reached, as main connections to and from the A3 autoroute can be made for Salerno and also Vietri. There are well-marked exit signs.

This is very much a business city and tourists are not often seen here. Accommodation and dining are geared to it's importance as a port and naval installation, so you will find that the hotels are rather modern and businesslike too.

Salerno
LUXURY
Hotel Jolly della Palma, Lungomare Trieste 1, tel: 089-225 222, fax: 089-237 571. A member of the international Jolly chain, this large, modern air-conditioned hotel, is situated on the water's edge. It is of good quality and offers 104 comfortable rooms. It is also near the beautiful gardens of the Villa Communale and other interesting sites.

MID-RANGE
Plaza Hotel, Vittorio Veneto 42, tel: 089-224 477, fax: 089-237 311, or e-mail: plaza@general.it
Central, this air-conditioned, 44-room hotel, is clean and simple. There is a bar, but unfortunately no dining room. The parking lot at the back of the hotel is a real advantage as the streets can get quite busy in the summer.
The Salerno, Via G Vicinanza 42, tel: 089-224 211, fax: 089-224 432. Just off the Corso Emmanuele, this is a small (17-room), plain, in-town hotel, with air conditioning.

BUDGET
Santa Rosa, Corso, V Emmanuele 16, tel/fax: 089-225 346. Not far from the station on the wide boulevard leading to the town centre. It is a very small hotel with facilities for the handicapped.
Youth Hostel, Via Luigi Guercio 112, tel: 089-790 251.

Paestum
There are hotels in nearby towns, and several simple pensiones and camping sites along the coast close to the site, though some only offer stopovers with meals. If you want to stay in Paestum and enjoy the sandy and rarely crowded beach, check the tourist information office for suggestions. (located close to the Paestum site entrance).

Salerno and Paestum at a Glance

MID-RANGE

Mec Paestum, at Licinela, Via Tiziano 23, tel: 0828-722 444, fax: 0828-722 305. A 54-room air-conditioned hotel with a lovely garden, swimming pool, a tenniscourt, private beach and a restaurant. There is also access for the disabled.

Cristallo, at Laura, Via P della Madonna 39, tel: 0828-851 077, fax: 0828-851 468. There are lovely gardens and a private beach at this 36-room hotel. Also restaurant-bar and disabled access.

Helios, tel: 0828-811 451. Situated close to the temples, with 30 rooms and a nice garden. There are also two restaurants that serve good seafood dishes.

Alternative accommodation

Tenuto Seliano, tel 0828 724 544. An unusual find, a farm in the local countryside mainly producing milk from buffalos to make mozarella. This farmhouse is for longer stays with meals offered, there is also a swimming pool and a lovely garden. At Capaccio, 14km (9 miles) from Paestum, the Aziendo Agricola scheme also has riding stables.

WHERE TO EAT

Again not a notable town for food, but plenty of small satisfactory restaurants along the main roads and nice little family places too, as well as the inevitable chain snackeries. For those who are self catering, there are many food shops and a market too. Try the **Apollo**, set in an atmospheric old house. Otherwise there are several other cheaper places to eat. It is probably better to visit a local market before you leave here, and go to the beach or the nearby woods, for an enjoyable picnic. *See* Cilento, below.

SHOPPING

Salerno has some surprisingly good small shops situated along the busy Corso V. Emanuele, which leads to the ancient town centre, with yet more smaller shops. It is very busy on weekends. Don't waste time and money on cheap stalls by the entrance to the site. On (or rather just off) site souvenir stalls can be very mediocre. Postcards can be alright though. Some Italian sites do have their own approved shops with excellent items, however. Otherwise it is better to wait and check the shops and art galleries in major towns where the quality should be a little better.

CILENTO

An unusual spot for lovers of the countryside is the Cilento, an area that extends into the sea just south of Paestum, and runs all the way to the neighbouring province of Basilicata to the south. A mountainous and wild place, it offers all sorts of possibilities for nature lovers' exploration – bird watching, and tracks for hiking, running and riding. On the whole it is a beautiful and unspoiled part of the country, especially inland, where there is a natural forest of ancient olive trees and chestnuts. The Cilento has a coastal area with reasonable hotels, especially for a short stay. Uncrowded small resorts along the beach edge are worth exploring for good value rooms and food.

TOURS AND EXCURSIONS

Paestum is not far from Salerno, closer to Agripoli in the south. Paestum is one of the most popular of the historic sites of Campania with Europe's finest Doric temples. There are plenty of possibilities for tours, mostly with guides. When visiting, allow for a whole day as there is lots to see here. Ask for details at tourist offices.

USEFUL CONTACTS

Tourist Offices
Salerno

Train Station, Piazza Vittorio Veneto, tel: 089-231 432.

Paestum

On the main road, at the entrance to the archaeological site, tel 0828-811 016.

Travel Tips

Tourist Information
Italian Tourist Offices
Canada, 1 Place Ville Marie Ste 1914, Quebec H3B 2C3, Montreal, tel: 514-866 0975/866 7669, fax: 514-392 1429, e-mail: initaly@ican.net
UK, 1 Princes St, London W1R 9AY, tel: 0207-408 1254, fax: 0207-493 6695, e-mail: italy@ italiantouristboard.co.uk
USA, 630 Fifth Ave, Ste 1565, New York 10111, NY, tel: 212-245 5095/245 4822, fax: 212-586 9249.
Official Tourism Website: www.enit.it
Embassies and Consulates
Australia, 12 Grey Street, Deakin, Canberra A C T 2600, tel: 06-273 3333, fax: 06-273 4223, e-mail: italembassy@netinfo.com.au
Canada, 275, Slater Street, 21st floor, Ottawa, Ontario K1P 5H9, tel: 613-232 2401/2/3 ,fax: 613- 233 1484, e-mail: italcomm@trytel.com
New Zealand, 34 Grant Road, Wellington, tel: 04-473 5339/ 472 9302, fax: 04-472 7255.
South Africa, 796 George Avenue, Arcadia, Pretoria, tel: 012-435 541/2/3/4/, fax: 012-435 547;

2 Grey's Pass, Gardens, Cape Town, tel: 021-235 157/8, fax: 021-240 146.
UK, 14 Three Kings Yard, London W1, tel: 0207-312 2200, fax: 0207-312 2230. Consulate, I38 Eaton Place London SW1X 8AN, tel: 0171-259 6322. Consulates also in **Edinburgh** and **Manchester**.
USA, 1601, Fuller St. N W, Washington D C, 20009, tel: 202-328 500/1/2/3/4/5/6/7/8, fax: 202-328 5593/462 3605. Consulates also in **Chicago**, **Los Angeles**, **New York**, and **San Francisco**.
Foreign Consulates in Naples
South Africa, Corso Umberto I, tel: 081-551 7519; **UK**, Via Francesco Crispi 122, tel: 0208-663 511, fax: 0208-761 3720; **USA**, Piazza della Repubblica, tel: 081-583 8111.

Entry Requirements
EU citizens need a national ID card; all other visitors require a valid passport. Visas are not required by any citizens of the Commonwealth or the USA for stays of up to three months. Other nationalities should check with the nearest embassy or consulate before travelling.

Customs and Entry Regulations
Italy is part of the European Union and standard EU customs allowances apply. Guidelines for goods bought duty-paid within the EU are 800 cigarettes, 400 cigarillos, 200 cigars, 10 litres of spirits, 20 litres of fortified wine, 90 litres of wine and 110 litres of beer. For duty-free or goods bought outside the EU, allowances are: 200 cigarettes or 100 cigarillos or 50 cigars or 250g tobacco; 1 litre of spirits or 2 litres of sparkling or fortified wine and 2 litres of still wine; 50g perfume or 250cc of toilet water.

Health
Italy is a healthy destination, with good food, clean water, few serious diseases, and excellent medical care. There is no need to have any inoculations. The water is safe, although mineral water is freely available. In high summer, take sunblock, a hat and drink plenty of fluids to counter the intense heat. There are reciprocal arrangements with all other EU countries and with Australia. UK citizens

should fill out form E111, available over post office counters.

If taken ill, ask at a pharmacy (identified by a green cross), as they are able to help with many minor ailments and prescribe a wide variety of medicines. Each town operates a rota for late night and weekend opening.

Farmacia Almasalus, Piazza Dante 71, tel: 081-549 9336, stays open 24 hours a day.

If you need a doctor, ask your hotel, or check the yellow pages under Unità Sanitaria. If in doubt, call the **Guardia Medica**, tel: 081-563 1111. **A&E departments (Pronto Soccorso)**, Ospedale Cardarelli, Via Cardarelli 9, tel: 081-747 2956; Ospedale dei Pellegrini, Via Portamedina 41, tel: 081-563 3234; and Ospedale San Paolo, Via Terracina 219; tel: 081-768 6284.

Insurance: It is advisable to take out comprehensive travel insurance to cover medical and other emergencies.

Transport

By Air: From London, there are direct scheduled services to Naples Capodichino Airport on British Airways and Go (central Booking tel: 0845-605 4321; website: www.go-fly.com). There are also charter flights in season, international departures from Paris, Brussels and Athens, and domestic flights from many other Italian airports. Naples Capodichino airport (tel: 081-789 6111) is about 10 minutes drive from the city centre. There is no rail connection, but taxis are plentiful, there are airport buses to Naples, Sorrento and Amalfi; while local buses no. 14 and 14r connect to Piazza Garibaldi, in central Naples. For airline offices in Naples try **Alitalia**, Via Medina 41, tel: 081-542 5222; **Aerolineas Argentinas**, Via Medina 40, tel: 081-552 0279; **Air France**, Via S. Carlo 34, tel: 081-552 2945; **Air Littoral c/o Air France Alisarda**, Via Depretis 78, tel: 081-552 6661; **British Airways**, Via Partenope 31, tel: 081-764 5550; **Iberia**, Via Ponte di Tappia 62, tel: 081-552 2080; **KLM**, Via S. Bartolomeo 63, tel: 081-552 3447; **Lufthansa**, Piazza Municipio 72, tel: 081-551 5440, **Meridiana Linée Aerée**, Via Depretis 78, tel: 081-551 9479; **Olympia Airways**, Via Cesario Console 2, tel: 081-764 8530; **Sabena**, Via Ponte di Tappia 47, tel: 081-551 2404; **SAS**, Via S. Giacomo 32, tel: 081-552 1059; **TWA**, Via Partenope 23, tel: 081-764 5828; **Varig**, Via De Pretis 108, tel: 081-704 6255.

By Train: There are excellent, frequent and remarkably affordable rail connections with the rest of Italy via Italian state railways, **Ferrovie dello Stato** (FS), with services to Rome at least once an hour (journey time: 2-3 hours, dependent on the type of train). You pay more for faster services and must have advance reservations on the fastest EC (Eurocity) services. A smaller number of international services connect via Milan or Rome. Validate your

ticket in the machine at the entrance to the platform before boarding. **Stazione Centrale**, Piazza Garibaldi; information tel: 1478-88088 (numero verde; open 07:00–21:00) is Naples' main station. Many of the trains from Rome also stop at **Campi Flegrei** and **Mergellina**.

There are plenty of local trains to Sorrento, Pompeii, along the northern arm of the bay to Pozzuoli and Cumae, north to Caserta and south to Salerno.

By Coach: There are coach services to all other major cities in Italy, and even a few international routes, such as the London–Naples direct service by National Express Eurolines (UK, tel: 0990-143 219). The main local coach operators include:

ACTP, Via Arenaccia 29, Naples, tel: 081-700 1111. Local services to the Vesuvius area and Caserta; departing from Piazza Capuana, near Piazza Garibaldi. **SEPSA**, Via

Cisterna dell'Olio 44, Naples, tel: 081-735 4197. Services to the Campi Flegrei; leaving from Piazza Garibaldi. **SITA**, Via Pisanelli 3-7, Naples, tel: 081-552 2176. Local services to the Sorrentine Peninsula and Amalfi Coast. ACTP and SEPSA; SITA services depart from the office in Via Pisanelli, near Piazza Municipio.

By Car: Italy's motorways are all toll roads, and can prove expensive, but credit card payments are accepted. Inner city driving in Naples is to be avoided at all costs, but there is a fast 20km (12-mile) ring road surrounding the city if you need to get past. Rural roads are well-built and reasonably empty; the exception is the Amalfi Drive which becomes one-way in summer to cope with the volume of traffic. EU drivers may use their national **license**; all others need an international driving permit. If you take in your own car, you will need a Green Card and it is sensible to take out extended breakdown cover or a reciprocal agreement with your national motoring organization. Keep all relevant papers, including the car's ownership documentation, in the car at all times. You may not need a car – public transport is excellent in the area. If you do, shop around, prices are high and very variable. To **hire a car** you must be at least 21 and have had a clean license for a full year.

Avis, Airport, tel: 081-780 5790; Via Piedigrotta 44, Naples tel: 081-761 1365;

Stazione Centrale, Piazza Garibaldi, tel: 081-554 3020. **Eurodollar**, Airport, tel: 081-780 2963; Via Partenope 13, tel: 081-764 6364. **Europcar**, Airport, tel: 081-780 5643; Via Scarfoglio 10, tel: 081-570 8426. **Hertz**, Airport, tel: 081-599 0924; Via Sauro 21, tel: 081-764 5323; Piazza Garibaldi 93, tel: 081-081 554 8657. **Italrent**, Airport, tel: 081-599 1316. **Interrentacar**, Via Partenope 37, tel: 081-764 5060. **Maggiore**, Airport, tel: 081-780 3011; Via Cervantes 92, tel: 081-552 1900; Stazione Centrale, Piazza Garibaldi, tel: 081-287 858.

Drive on the right and give way to the left. **Speed limits** for normal cars are 50kph (30mph) in built-up areas, 110kph (70mph) on rural roads, and 130kph (80mph) on motorways. Drinking and driving is strictly forbidden with on-the-spot penalties. There are 24 hour **fuel service stations** at Piazza Carlo III, Via Foria, Piazza Municipio, and Piazza Mergellina. There are **car parks** at **Parcheggio di interscambio**, Via Benedetto Brin, tel: 081-763 2832; **Garage dei Fiori**, Via Colonna 21, tel: 081-414 190; **Grilli**, Via Ferraris 40, tel: 081-264 344; **Mergellina**, Via Mergellina 112, tel: 081-761 3470; **Sannazaro**, Piazza Sannazzaro 142, tel: 081-681 437; **Santa Chiara**, Pallonetto Santa Chiara 30, tel: 081-551 6303; **Supergarage**, Via Shelley 11, tel: 081-551 3104; **Turistico**,

Via De Gasperi, tel: 081-552 5442.

If you are in an **accident**, place a warning triangle 50m (164ft) behind the car and call the police (tel: 112 or 113). Exchange names, addresses and insurance details with other parties and witnesses. Do not admit or imply liability until you have had a chance to think clearly and take advice. If you **breakdown**, tel: 116 and give your location, car registration and make. **The Automobile Club d'Italia** (24 hour emergency, tel: 06-4477) will come to the rescue. This can be expensive unless you have breakdown cover.

By Ferry: Naples has regular ferry connections with Cagliari, Sardinia (Tirrenia, tel: 081-720 1111); Palermo and Milazzo; Sicily (Tirrenia, tel: 081-720 1111; SNAV, tel: 081-761 2348; SIREMAR, tel: 081-580 0340/720 1595) and Tunis (Linee Lauro, tel: 081-551 3352).

Money Matters

Currency: The old Italian currency (the lira) has now been replaced by the single European currency, the euro. It is divided into 100 cents. Notes are available in denominations of 5, 10, 20, 50, 100, 200 and 500 euros and coins in 1, 2, 5, 10, 20 and 50 euro cents and 1 and 2 euros. Many prices are still marked in lire, beside the euro amount.

Credit cards: All major credit cards are widely accepted. Eurocheques are not recommended.

Exchange: Banks tend to cluster in certain areas, such as near Piazza Municipio and behind Via Partenope. Not all have exchange facilities, queues can be long and ID is required for all transactions. Most now have ATM machines that can be used with either a credit card or your normal cheque guarantee card. The exchange booth in the Stazione Centrale stays open daily 07:00–21:00.

Thomas Cook, Piazza Municipio 70, tel: 081-551 8399.

Tipping: When tipping hotel staff, tip about 50c to one euro for the porter, doorman or room service. About the same, per day, for the chambermaid. In restaurants there is usually a 10–15 per cent service charge on the bill, but it is customary to leave a little more small change. For taxis, tip about 10 per cent, and at bars: it is customary to give a small tip, often at the start of the evening, to ensure good service. When at the cinema, give cinema ushers a few coins. Also give a small tip to any custodian who opens a locked area or church for you while you are visiting sights. Tour guides should be given around three euros. You can give toilet attendants small coins.

Children

Children are very welcome everywhere and actually act as an excellent form of introduction to the locals. Take them out to dinner with you in the evening; children under four years get free transport

and museum entry and half-price from 4–12 years.

Disabled Visitors

People are willing to help, but most facilities are poor and the area has steep hills and steps, cobbled streets and large areas with no access for cars. It is possible to get around, but will require careful planning. For information try: **UK: RADAR** (Royal Association for Disability and Rehabilitation), 12 City Forum, 250 City Road, London EC1V 8AF, tel: (0207) 250 3222, fax: (0207) 250 1212. Holiday Care Service, 2nd Floor, Imperial Buildings, Victoria Rd, Horley, Surrey RH6 7PZ, tel: 01293-774 535. **USA:** SATH (Society for the Advancement of Travel for the Handicapped), 347 Fifth Ave, Ste 610, New York NY10016, tel: 212-447 7284, fax: 212-725 8253. Mobility International USA, PO Box 10767, Eugene, Oregon 97440, tel: 541-343 1284.

Business Hours

Banks open Monday–Friday 08:30–13:00 and for one hour in the afternoon (usually

15:00–16:00). **Post Offices** are open Monday–Saturday, 08:30–19:30; smaller branches usually open Monday–Friday, 08:30–17:00; Saturday 08.30– 12:00. **Shops** are open Monday–Saturday, 08:00/ 09:00–13:00, 16:00–19:00/20:00. More now opening on Sundays. For **Museums** and sights: see individual entries. Tourist Office hours vary, but standard times are Monday–Saturday, 09:00–13:00, 16:00–19:00.

Time Difference

GMT +1 in winter; GMT +2 in summer. The time changes in late March and September.

Communications

Stamps (*francobolli*) are available from hotels, newsagents and tobacconists and post offices. There is usually a small charge for collecting *Poste restante* mail. There are many fax offices and internet cafés. The **telephone** system works well and most international phone cards and 'Country Direct' numbers are recognized. Tariffs are cheapest between 22:00 and 08:00

CONVERSION CHART		
FROM	**TO**	**MULTIPLY BY**
Millimetres	Inches	0.0394
Metres	Yards	1.0936
Metres	Feet	3.281
Kilometres	Miles	0.6214
Kilometres square	Square miles	0.386
Hectares	Acres	2.471
Litres	Pints	1.760
Kilograms	Pounds	2.205
Tonnes	Tons	0.984
To convert Celsius to Fahrenheit: x 9 ÷ 5 + 32		

Italian grammar and pronunciation are both logical, but there are a few things to remember. 'C' is hard (e.g. 'cat') unless followed by an 'I' or 'E', when it becomes 'Ch' (e.g. 'chair'). 'G' is hard (e.g. 'goat') unless softened by 'I' or 'E' (e.g. 'gerbil'). 'CC' is the equivalent to the English 'CH' (e.g. 'church'). 'CH' at the beginning of a word is pronounced as a hard 'G' (e.g. 'guitar').

Good morning/afternoon or evening/night • *Buon giorno/Buona sera/Buona notte*
Hello/Bye (informal) • *Ciao*
Goodbye • *Arrivaderci*
Yes • *Si*
No • *No*
Please • *Per favore*
Thank you (very much) • *Grázie (molte)*
Excuse me • *Mi scusi/prego*
Excuse me (in a crowd) • *Permesso*
You're welcome • *Prego*
Do you speak English? • *Parla inglese?*
I don't understand • *Non ho capito*
I don't know • *No lo so*
I'm sorry • *Mi dispiace*
Gentlemen/Ladies • *Signori/Signore*
Where is... ? • *Dov'è... ?*
When... ? • *Quando ... ?*
What is... ? • *Cos'è... ?*
How much is it? • *Quanto costa?*
Danger • *Pericolo*
Beware • *Attenzione*
No smoking • *Vietato fumare*
Left/right • *A sininstra/A destra*
Entrance/exit • *Entrata/uscita*
Open/closed • *Aperto/chiuso*

on weekdays, and all day on Sunday. Public phone boxes use credit cards or phone cards (*schede telefoniche*), sold at newsagents and tobacconists. Coin operated booths use tokens (gettoni). For international calls, look for a phone booth (*telefono a scatti*) in which you can pay for the call at the end. Most people seem to have mobile phones and GSM mobile phones will work (US and Japanese phones may not). For an operator dial 15, for an International operator (Intercontinental) dial 170, for local directory enquiries dial 12. For International directory enquiries dial 176. For reverse charge calls dial 172, followed by the country code. To direct dial abroad 00. Italy's country code (from abroad) is 39

Electricity

220V AC, 50 cycles. Most plugs have two round pins; a few have three round pins. Take a travel adapter.

Weights and Measures

Italy uses the metric system.

Personal Safety

Naples has a poor reputation for crime, but it really isn't that bad. Many of the headlines are made by high level corruption and crime which will not affect tourists. There is a fair amount of petty street crime in certain areas (particularly around the station and the docks). Be careful where you walk alone, especially at night, and keep track of wallets, bags and phones. It is advisable to keep

separate reference copies of all vital documents.
There are several different police forces. The **Vigili Urbana** (town police) handle traffic and parking offences in town; the **Polizia Stradale** deal with motorway traffic offences. The **Carabinieri** is responsible for general crime, but thefts should be reported to the **Polizia Statale**. Police headquarters, Via Medina 75, tel: 081-794 1111.

Emergencies

For general **emergency** tel: 113. Also call the **police**: 112, **fire**: 115, **ambulance**: 081-752 0696 (24 hrs)/081-752 0850 (day only), **car breakdown**: 116, **coast guard** 081-206 118/9 or 081-206 133/231.

NUMBERS

1 • uno
2 • due
3 • tre
4 • quattro
5 • cinque
6 • sei
7 • sette
8 • otto
9 • nove
10 • dieci
11 • undici
12 • dodici
13 • tredici
14 • quattordici
20 • venti
30 • trenta
40 • quaranta
50 • cinquante
60 • sessanta
70 • settanta
80 • ottanta
90 • novanta
100 • cento
1000 • mille

INDEX